D0008336

WHO IS

JESUS

. . . REALLY?

[A DIALOGUE ON GOD, MAN, AND GRACE]

COFFEE · HOUSE

CHRONICLES

WHO IS

JESUS

. . . REALLY?

JOSH MCDOWELL
AND DAVE STERRETT

MOODY PUBLISHERS
CHICAGO

All Scripture quotations, unless otherwise indicated, are taken from the *Holy Bible, New International Version*®, NIV®. Copyright ©1973, 1978, 1984 by Biblica, Inc.™ Used by permission of Zondervan. All rights reserved worldwide.

All Scripture quotations marked NASB are taken from the *New American Standard Bible*®, Copyright © 1960, 1962, 1963, 1968, 1971, 1972, 1973, 1975, 1977, 1995 by The Lockman Foundation. Used by permission. (www.Lockman.org)

All Scripture quotations marked NLT are taken from the *Holy Bible, New Living Translation*, copyright © 1996, 2004. Used by permission of Tyndale House Publishers, Inc., Wheaton, Illinois 60189, U.S.A. All rights reserved.

All Scripture quotations marked KJV are taken from the King James Version.

Edited by Paul Santhouse
Interior design: Ragont Design
Sterrett Photo: Katherine Robertson
McDowell Photo: Barbara Gannon

Cover design: Faceout Studio
Cover image: Getty #71854369, and
    iStock #8196668, #6032134

Library of Congress Cataloging-in-Publication Data

McDowell, Josh.
  Who is Jesus—really? : a dialogue on God, man, and grace / Josh McDowell and Dave Sterrett.
    p. cm. — (The coffeehouse chronicles ; 2)
  Includes bibliographical references.
  ISBN 978-0-8024-8767-4
  1. Jesus Christ—Person and offices. 2. Jesus Christ—Historicity.
3. Apologetics. I. Sterrett, Dave. II. Title.
BT203.M3387 2011
232'.8—dc22   2010042290

This is a work of fiction. Names, characters, places, and incidents either are the product of the authors' imagination or are used fictitiously, and any resemblance to actual persons, living or dead, businesses, companies, events, or locales is entirely coincidental.

All websites and phone numbers listed herein are accurate at the time of publication, but may change in the future or cease to exist. The listing of website references and resources does not imply publisher endorsement of the site's entire contents. Groups and organizations are listed for informational purposes, and listing does not imply publisher endorsement of their activities.

We hope you enjoy this book from Moody Publishers. Our goal is to provide high-quality, thought-provoking books and products that connect truth to your real needs and challenges. For more information on other books and products written and produced from a biblical perspective, go to www.moodypublishers.com or write to:

Moody Publishers
820 N. LaSalle Boulevard
Chicago, IL 60610

1 3 5 7 9 10 8 6 4 2

Printed in the United States of America

To

Dr. Robert Saucy,
my professor and mentor for three years.
Who always challenged me to love Jesus,
study the Scriptures, and pursue Truth.
—Josh

To

David Gilbert, Michael Gilbert, and Bill Sterrett
These three men, who love Christ,
have challenged me to share God's love with others.
—Dave

CONTENTS

One

COFFEEHOUSE SHOWDOWN

Late September
Opal School of Religion
Dallas, TX

THE AUDITORIUM was packed. Hundreds of students, faculty, and donors turned out for the humanitarian dinner, and Dr. William Peterson, professor emeritus at Opal School of Religion, was about to deliver the keynote. He walked onstage to hearty applause, spread his notes on the lectern, and made eye contact with friends.

"Thank you for that very gracious welcome. Honestly, the students who organized this event deserve all the recognition, and I'll be asking one of them to join me up here in just a moment. First, let me highlight an important upcoming event here at the school of religion.

"We're pleased to announce an exciting new lecture series entitled 'The Historical Christ: Will the Real Jesus Please Stand Up.' Beginning October 8, right here in Wesley Auditorium, three professors—including two of our own—will be exploring and debating the historicity of Jesus Christ. This is something you won't want to miss."

Nick, sitting at a front table, nodded at his friend and instructor, Jamal Washington. Jamal would be one of those speakers, and Nick couldn't wait.

Dr. Peterson went on to recognize several teams of students who spent their summer months working with orphans and refugees in Majority World countries. Then, turning to his right, he invited one of them, Jessica Friesen, to join him at the podium and describe this year's student-led humanitarian campaign. Nick's heart pounded as Jessica crossed the stage. She looked *stunning.* He noted how long her hair looked when she wore it down, and how fit she looked, probably from her marathon training. *If only I'd acted differently she might still be interested in me,* he mused. *Maybe I should have . . . huh?* His friend Jared was shoving a note under his elbow. He unfolded it and read, "Hey—close your mouth, chump!"

Nick smiled at him, and then turned back toward Jessica. She had been completely transformed since coming to faith in Christ five months ago. All she ever talked about was Jesus. No more getting wasted with the girls at the bars on McKinney and Lower Greenville. She even turned him down one night when he asked her out for Tex-Mex. What was that about? She *loved* Tex-Mex. Nick was offended because her rejection seemed personal. Although she expressed genuine gratitude for his influence in leading her to trust Christ, the more she grew in her relationship with God, the less time she made for her relationship with him.

Then again, she *was* busy. Between her nineteen credit hours, leading the Sudan project for girls, and training for the marathon, the only time he saw her was at the weekly *I am Second* campus Bible study. He shook his head. Months ago he was the one resisting a romantic relationship because of her disinterest in Christianity. Now she was avoiding him! It just didn't make sense.

Jessica closed with a story about the Opal students who had traveled to Sudan during the summer. The audience was moved by her emotional appeal and responded with a round of applause and cheering as she returned to her seat.

Throughout Dr. Peterson's lecture Nick glanced at Jessica and reflected on their times together. At one point, her eyes met his and she smiled before quickly looking back at Professor Peterson. She seemed to be moving on, and Nick felt convicted that he should be thinking more about the children in Sudan.

Two

JESUS CHANGING ROCK STARS

IT WAS TUESDAY NIGHT and two hundred students were packed into McCulloch Coffee House for the weekly *I am Second* Bible study. Following a strong set of worship songs from the band, Nick mounted the stage while everyone else found seats. He wore a black T-shirt with bold white letters proclaiming *I am Second*. Grabbing the microphone he spoke with clarity and confidence. "I *am* second, and so are you! We're second because *Jesus Christ is first*!" At these simple words the students broke out in applause. One thing was for certain—this group didn't lack for enthusiasm.

Nick continued, "Before we show this

week's video, I'm going to read you one of the all-time greatest descriptions of Jesus Christ ever written. It's from the apostle Paul's letter to the Colossians."

> He is the image of the invisible God, the firstborn over all creation. For by him all things were created: things in heaven and on earth, visible and invisible, whether thrones or powers or rulers or authorities; all things were created by him and for him. He is before all things, and in him all things hold together. And he is the head of the body, the church; he is the beginning and the firstborn from among the dead, so that in everything he might have the supremacy. For God was pleased to have all his fullness dwell in him, and through him to reconcile to himself all things, whether things on earth or things in heaven, by making peace through his blood, shed on the cross.[1]

As soon as Nick finished reading, Jessica stepped onstage and led the students in a prayer. On her "amen," the lights dimmed and the *I am Second* video began. Nick was pumped. *This powerful story was bound to get some feedback!*

The video kicked off with eerie music in a totally dark room. A weird light shone over a white chair, and the voice of Brian "Head" Welch, former lead guitarist for the band Korn, came from off camera. Then he was sitting in the chair, surrounded by darkness, and covered with tattoos—including a tattoo of a small cross outside his right eye. The students were silent as Welch told his story with great sincerity.

"There was a few times where life seemed good. My daughter Jenna came into the world and it was just such a euphoric feeling. I thought my life could just feel like that forever. I thought I was 'spiritual,' but I couldn't stay sober. I hit rock bottom. I'd sworn that I would never do methamphetamines again because I saw what it did to my child's mother. It just took my wife's feelings away and made her leave her kid. I just wanted my wife dead. I wanted to kill her. I thought she was the scum of the earth. How could she do drugs like that and let the drugs win her like that? So I was never going to do meth again.

"I ended up with an everyday crippling addiction to methamphetamine and everything that I said about my ex-wife came true for me. I sunk to the lowest gutter I could ever think of. I would spend time with my kid and I would still be on it because I needed it to function. I would get up in the morning and have a peanut butter and jelly sandwich and snort meth and then take her to school. I was a junkie. My life was just spinning out of control. Jenna had come out on one of the tours. I just remember her skipping around singing one of our Korn songs called 'A.D.I.D.A.S.' 'All Day I Dream About Sex.' And I'm going like, 'What am I doing? I'm a junkie, my daughter is singing all day I dream about sex, and I'm going to die.'

"My real estate broker, Eric, said, 'Brian, I don't mean to be weird with you, I hope you don't take this the wrong way, but I felt the Scripture jump out at me. I've never done this before so I don't really know how to do this, but I felt like this would mean something to you. It's Matthew 11:28. Jesus says, "Come to me all who are weary and burdened and I will give you rest."'

"I remember, all tweaked out, looking up in the dictionary 'weary.' I looked up 'burdened' and I pulled the Scripture apart. I admitted, 'I'm wearied and burdened and I need rest for my soul.' I didn't know if it was real, but they invited me to church a couple weeks later and I said a prayer to receive Christ at the church but I went home just like

I used to do. I neglected my daughter, got it all smooth and powdery. But before I took it, I prayed, 'Jesus, You gotta take these drugs from me. Search me right now. Search my heart.'

"Something happened. I felt so much fatherly love from heaven and it was like 'I don't condemn you. I love you. I love you.' It was just love and instantly that love from God came into me. It was so powerful that the next day I threw away all my drugs and I quit Korn. I said, 'I'm quitting Korn and I'm going to raise my kid the right way.' I got the love from God coming into me and then it came out of me to my kid. It changed me. My heart was changed and I said to my daughter, 'Jenna, Daddy's going to be home with you all the time. I'm quitting my career.' And her face lit up and she was like, 'for me?' She felt so special and God used her to save me . . . to save her life later on."[2]

Nick returned to the stage as the lights came back up. He had a small leather Bible in his hand and chose his words carefully. "Maybe you too feel weary and burdened. If we're all willing to be honest, most of us have felt wearied.

Last year, at least for me, it was late nights, hangovers, and some serious confusion about my life. Even now I struggle between having fun and doing well in school . . . not to mention that I'm totally addicted to caffeine. Every student knows what it's like to be burdened, and to carry heavy loads. If that's you right now, here's something you should know. You don't have to figure it all out before coming to Jesus.

"Maybe you can relate to Brian Welch. Meth is a tough master. But so is drinking too much, or doing *anything* too much. You heard what he said about how to gain your freedom.

"Or maybe you watched that entire video and thought, 'I may not be perfect, but I don't have *any* problems like *that* guy had. I'm a good person living a good life and I'm good with God. Why surrender my life to Jesus?'

"Let me ask you a couple of questions. Have you ever told a lie?" Nick smiled. "Yeah, me too. The trouble is, that makes you and me *liars*. Have you ever had lust in your heart? How about your eyes—ever looked with lust at someone? Jesus said that anyone who lusts has committed adultery in his heart. Before I came to Jesus last year I looked at pornography all the time. Believe me, I know what it's like to get wasted and treat girls disrespectfully. How about this—have you ever hated anyone? Jesus said anyone who hates his brother or sister has committed murder in his heart. That makes every one of us a lying, adulterous murderer. You can check all this out in the gospel of Matthew, chapter five.

"We've all done lots of good things, and most of us live with the best of intentions. But compared to the infinite goodness and holiness of a Perfect Being, our best actions will never measure up. There's only one way to be good enough to stand before a holy God. You have to let Him forgive you. Today can be the day you receive Christ. He paid for your sin with His death. Accept that gift and make Him first in your life.

"Now is the perfect time to make a decision about Jesus. We're not promised tomorrow. Let's suppose hypothetically that you leave here tonight and get hit by a drunk driver. As you stand before God to give an account of your life, will you stand guilty . . . or innocent? Do you think you would go to heaven . . . or hell? If you don't know Jesus, I encourage you to talk with Him right now. Confess your sin, accept His forgiveness, and give Him control over your life. He died in your place and will forgive you and cleanse you of all of your sin!"

Three

THE SURPRISE

THE INSTANT NICK finished speaking, a former friend and classmate stood up and shouted, "That's just *your* opinion, Nick!" She was wearing a bright T-shirt proclaiming *There's Probably No God—Now Stop Worrying and Enjoy Your Life* in bold letters, and everyone stared.

Nick was startled, but recovered quickly. "Andrea? What are you doing? And what do you mean by that? You know what I've said is more than just my opinion. Every bit of it corresponds to historical reality. On what foundation is your opinion based?"

Immediately another student stood up, this one wearing a black shirt with

Atheist printed in red letters. "Jesus Christ was a man! Nothing more! What makes you think your Jesus is better than any other teacher?"

Nick turned to look at him and said, "You're right—Jesus *was* a man. But He was also God, and He proved His claims of deity by His resurrection."

Another student yelled, "Hey Nick, you're full of it!"

Nick, growing irritated, called back, "What's your name?"

The student didn't answer, so Nick persisted. "You—the one who told me I'm full of it. What's your name?"

Lord, give Nick wisdom, Jessica prayed silently.

"I'm Sam," replied the student.

"Okay, Sam. Explain to me how I'm full of it."

"Jesus Christ was just a man . . . and that's all. A do-good teacher followed by some misguided, naïve people—like you. Those people attributed outrageous supernatural abilities to Him."

Nick shot back, "Why do you think so many people attributed supernatural power to Him?"

Sam didn't answer because the guy with the atheist T-shirt, cut in. "Very few, if any, books written back then mentioned His divinity. Jesus might have been a popular guy, but He sure wasn't divine."

Nick was in adrenaline mode. "You really don't have any basis for your claim—and I was actually asking Sam the question."

Sam yelled, "Jesus wasn't even a good teacher! He was a moron on a power trip, deceiving the gullible with riddles and condemning anyone who disagreed to hell."

Nick looked at Sam. "First of all, you're contradicting yourself. You just said Jesus was a 'do-good teacher.' You also said He was a moron who taught riddles, yet the people attributed supernatural abilities to Him. If Jesus was just an ignorant moron, why would eyewitnesses attribute miracles to Him?"

"You're just a superstitious Christian!" yelled another angry student. "We don't believe in God, talking snakes, virgin births, or unicorns!"

Things were getting out of hand. *Did Andrea bring the entire atheist club here just to interrupt me?* wondered Nick. Then he got an idea. "Friends, I understand why some of you are angry. I felt the same way as an agnostic. I couldn't even stand the thought of God. I get that. But we're running out of time here so let me make a request. I ask that you not interrupt tonight's meeting any more. We can have dialogue without verbal attacks. In fact, in three weeks we're hosting a forum with one of our own instructors, Jamal Washington, addressing the identity of the historical Christ. Jamal, a theist, will be joined by Dr. Jurgen Hitzfield, the agnostic church historian, and Dr. Franck Gouffran, an atheist philosopher of science. I invite you to come to this forum. For now, I'm going to close in prayer and then the band is going to close us out with a couple more songs. I ask that you would please be respectful and not interrupt me. Also, Andrea, will you chat with me afterwards?"

Andrea's face remained blank, and when the band finished up she was gone. Nick hoped either Mina or Jessica connected with her, but it seemed like she was hurting and didn't want to talk.

He left the coffeehouse frustrated that he hadn't offered better answers and that he didn't handle the rowdy crowd very well. He also felt convicted because of his bad attitude.

As he was leaving, a young man holding a motorcycle helmet stopped him. "Hey Nick, my name is Brett. Can I ask you a question?"

"Sure!"

"I liked the *I am Second* video, but do you think I can meet with you sometime about this stuff?"

"Yeah, I'd be glad to meet with you. Tell me what's up."

"First, I want to apologize for my rude atheist friends. I have my own questions and doubts, but they shouldn't have jacked your meeting."

"That's okay," said Nick. "Christians can be pretty rude sometimes, too."

Brett nodded. "Anyways, I'm a biology and premed student and I tend to be logical in my thinking. I didn't grow up in Texas like these Bible-thumping kids. My father taught at MIT and he trained us to avoid blind emotional faith.

Even though Brian Welch's story is good, I don't think personal testimony counts for much. Stories like his have no actual value to anyone but Christians, and such things only serve to strengthen what you guys already believe. It's confirmation bias."

"What you're saying makes sense," said Nick. "I would agree that personal testimony may not be the strongest intellectual argument for God, but I wouldn't say it doesn't have any actual value in reality."

"Nick, it matters to you because you're a Christian, but it doesn't count for anything to people like me who have a logical, rational, scientific outlook."

Nick motioned toward the outdoor tables and chairs. "You have a minute to talk?"

Four

A SKEPTIC WANTS HISTORICAL EVIDENCE

"NICK, IF I GAVE YOU a video of Mother Teresa expressing her doubts and how she could never feel God in her life, would you change your view? If not, you prove my point. Look, you could show me a video of Richard Dawkins himself becoming a Christian and saying, 'I am second to Jesus,' and it wouldn't impress me a bit. Like Christopher Hitchens said, the gospels have 'multiple authors—none of whom published anything until many decades after the Crucifixion and who cannot agree on anything of importance.'[3] Nick, if you really want me to believe in this Jesus of yours, you'll have to provide historical evidence. Even then I'll be skeptical of all the so-called miracles and 'Jesus is God' stuff."

"Why would you be skeptical if I provided historical evidence?" asked Nick.

"Because historical evidence would only prove Christ was a man of history, which is questionable. Like Bertrand Russell said, 'Historically, it's quite doubtful if Christ ever existed at all and if he did, we know very little about him.'"[4]

"Brett, I'm sure you know that Russell was a mathematician, not a historian. I even think Hitchens avoids a lot of historical evidence because of his anti-supernatural bias. And regardless of what Hitchens and Russell say, there actually *is* overwhelming evidence that Christ was a man of history. I'm happy to talk with you about it, but I'm no expert. Less than a year ago I was still a skeptic, and I'm pretty sure I won't be able to answer all of your questions. Would you be open to meeting with a couple of my friends as well? They helped me in my search for answers last year."

Brett picked up his helmet. "I might meet them. Why do you think they'll give better answers than you?"

"They've been researching this longer than I have. Jamal is working on his doctorate and teaching undergraduate courses. Mina is a first-year law student with a philosophy degree. She's already been published, and she's brilliant. Andrea knows them both, so maybe you could ask her to join us . . . along with some of her atheist friends." Nick smiled. "We meet at Caruth Haven Coffeehouse on

Wednesday nights. Does tomorrow night work with your schedule?"

"It works. I'll call my grad student friends from the atheist club and ask them to join us."

That evening, Nick called Jessica, Jamal, and Mina. Brett called Scott, a doctoral student in history, and Lauren, a third-year medical student. They all agreed to come.

Five

ANDREA

AFTER NICK'S CALL, Jessica and Mina prayed for Andrea to be open to joining the group the next night. Mina prayed, "Lord, show Andrea how much You love her. Show her that You know her personally, and that You are passionate about a relationship with her. Heavenly Father, Andrea has been hurt and now she's decided not to believe in You. Please open her heart and mind. In Jesus' name, Amen."

Over the summer Andrea had shifted to complete atheism, and she lost her interest in having spiritual discussions with Nick, Jamal, Mina, and Jessica. Nick wondered if it had anything to do with the

death of her cousin several months ago, but Andrea said it had to do with waking up to reality. Nick still cared about her as a friend, and he, Jessica, and Mina continued trying to hang out with Andrea. Two Sundays ago, Andrea had joined them at Jamal's house to watch the football game. She seemed more relaxed than usual, but they hadn't really talked about God much either.

Six

WEDNESDAY NIGHT AT THE CARUTH HAVEN COFFEEHOUSE

THE CARUTH HAVEN Coffeehouse is the largest coffee shop in Dallas. Yet, even with four spacious rooms and a patio it's filled with college students all the time. Even at 2:00 a.m. it's not uncommon to see graduate students studying, or drunk undergrads sobering up after the clubs shut down.

Jamal showed up a few minutes late and heads turned as he walked in. The college girls thought he was good looking and they smiled at each other. When Jamal finally approached their table, coffee in hand, Nick introduced everyone. Andrea had arrived with Mina and Jessica, and Brett brought his

atheist friends, Scott and Lauren. Nick felt a little intimidated being the youngest one there, but he was also eager
to learn from their interaction. "The reason we're all here
is because my brand-new friend, Brett, requested a conversation about Jesus Christ as a man of history. I don't feel
equipped to answer questions on that topic so I asked Jamal
and Mina to join us since they helped me with my own
questions last year. Brett, why don't you kick us off by
explaining what's on your mind."

"Sure." Addressing Jamal, Brett said, "I had mentioned
to Nick that prominent atheists like the late Bertrand Russell and Christopher Hitchens openly doubt the historicity
of Jesus Christ. Hitchens even refers to His existence as
'highly questionable.'[5] How do we really know that Christ
existed?"

"Good question, Brett. Let me explain why I believe
both Hitchens and Russell are mistaken. While historians
have debated whether some other figures of ancient times,
like Homer, existed at all, there is general unanimity that
Christ was a real person. If one believes in the existence of
Socrates, Alexander the Great, or Julius Caesar, then one
should definitely believe in Christ's existence. If historicity
is established by written records in multiple copies that
date originally from near contemporaneous sources, there
is far more historical evidence for Christ's existence than for
any of theirs. The historicity of Christ is attested not only

by Christians but also by Greek, Roman, and Jewish Sources."[6]

Lauren, Brett's friend from medical school, leaned forward and set her drink on the table. "Wait a second. I thought with you Christians it was all about faith."

Jamal responded, "Lauren, there's no question that many Christians have blind faith. Thankfully, it wasn't that way with the great thinkers like Anselm and Aquinas. The foundation of the Christian faith is a real event—the historical resurrection of Jesus Christ. Paul wrote to the Christians in the city of Corinth, 'If Christ has not been raised, our preaching is useless and so is your faith.'"[7]

Jamal continued, "Brett, Dr. Otto Betz, a brilliant historian, once remarked, 'No serious scholar has ventured to postulate the non-historicity of Jesus.'"[8]

"Jamal," Andrea cut in. "It really doesn't matter if Jesus was a man of history or not. Even if He existed, He wasn't God. He was just a great teacher or some fanatic."

Sounds like Andrea is spending too much time with Sam, thought Nick.

"Okay, Andrea, let's follow that track for a minute. You referred to Jesus Christ as a great teacher *or* some fanatic. Let's consider Him as a teacher. He was actually a profound philosopher and communicator. The early apologists held that the beauty and brilliance of His teaching surpassed Socrates, Plato, and Aristotle. I agree with the observations of Stanford research scholar Dinesh D'Souza, who pointed out that even though Shakespeare is the greatest dramatist of the English language, 'There is no single character in Shakespeare who can match Christ's eloquence.'[9] Think of all the popular expressions that were spoken by Christ. *By their fruits you shall know them. For where your treasure is, there your heart will be also. Forgive us our trespasses as we forgive those who trespass against us. Turn the other cheek. Man does not live by bread alone. Blessed are the meek, for they will inherit the earth. Whoever finds his life will lose it, and whoever loses his life for my sake will find it.*"[10]

Scott, the doctoral student, interrupted. "Jamal, maybe Jesus was a good teacher, but as I've studied history, I think society would be better off without Christ's followers. When I think about the impact Christianity has had on society, I think of fighting in the name of religion, hatred toward women and minority groups, and their attempts to stifle the advancement of science and academia."

"There's no question that evil things have been done and defended in the name of Christ," said Jamal. "Scott, let me ask you a question. Do you believe the human race is good or evil?"

"Good, for the most part," responded Scott. "I think your God is the one who is evil."

Andrea flipped open her laptop. "Scott, I agree with you. It's God and religion that are the source of evil. Jamal and Nick, let me read you one of my favorite quotes from

Richard Dawkins. This is from his book *The God Delusion.*
You've probably heard it. 'The God of the Old Testament
is arguably the most unpleasant character in all fiction;
jealous and proud of it; a petty, unjust, unforgiving con-
trol-freak; a vindictive, bloodthirsty ethnic cleanser; a
misogynistic, homophobic, racist, infanticidal, genocidal,
filicidal, pestilential, megalomaniacal, sadomasochistic,
capriciously malevolent bully.'"[11]

Mina spoke up. "Andrea, it sounds to me like you would
agree with most 'New Atheists' that human beings are basically good. Am I right?"

Andrea nodded.

"I don't see how that adds up logically. For example, if
Richard Dawkins is saying that this evil being called God
is merely fictional, then who is responsible for the evils of
religion? If God doesn't exist in reality, then it's mankind
who creates these evil religions. Why would you get angry
at God if He's just a fictional character? And how can you
justify the goodness of mankind after all the killing that
has happened throughout history?"

"Because most of the killing is done by those who
believe in God!"

"Actually, that's not historically true," Mina quickly
responded. "But let's set that aside for a minute and suppose
that *every* murder in history was performed by a person
believing in God. What basis does the atheist have for

optimism? Those murders are still done by *people*—by the human race—regardless of what fiction they believe."

"I think we need to embrace science, not God," commented Lauren.

"Why not both?" asked Mina. "I love science but it has limitations. Science can make observations about the physical world, but it can't answer simple questions about morality or goodness. Has the advancement of science helped us to become more peaceful over the past one hundred years? Not hardly. Throughout history humans continue to do evil things to one another. Perhaps this is why atheist Stephen Hawking believes that in order for the human race to survive, we should spread out to other planets."

"Might not be a bad idea," said Andrea.

Mina continued, "Andrea, getting back to your comment about most of the killing being done by those who believe in God, you'd want to consider what took place over the past hundred years. The atheist regimes of Stalin, Hitler, and Mao murdered more than one hundred million people. The deaths by religious zealots over hundreds of years is less than one percent of those done by the evils of atheism.[12] I know there are atheist bloggers who say that Hitler was a Christian, but historically this is nonsense. Hitler himself said, 'Through the peasantry we shall be able to destroy Christianity.'[13] In fact, he blamed the Jews for inventing Christianity."

"I understand that Hitler wasn't a real Christian," said Scott. "I'm guessing my atheist blogger friends are referring to his "I am fighting for the work of the Lord" passage in *Mein Kampf*.[14] Pretty convincing until you realize it's all propaganda designed to sway the masses. Even so, I believe the world would be better off without Christianity."

"I'm surprised to hear you say that, Scott," responded Mina. "As a student of history, surely you know how much good has happened in the name of Christianity."

"Jesus and His followers have contributed nothing good to society," snapped Andrea.

"Come on, Andrea, everyone knows that's not true," said Mina. "Even Dawkins admits that science was birthed out of religion. The late Dr. D. James Kennedy, who earned his PhD from New York University, documented in one of his books that if Christ had never been born, our world would be quite different.[15]

"First, Christianity has elevated the value of human life. For example, in classical Rome and Greece, infanticide was not only legal, it was applauded by some leaders! It was the early Christian church that ultimately brought an end to infanticide. Christianity has consistently held a high view of children—even unborn children."

"There you go with your pro-life talk," interjected Lauren. "Christianity doesn't value human life—it disgraces women and always has."

"That's not completely accurate, Lauren," said Mina. "Scott, feel free to correct me if I'm wrong here, but in ancient cultures, a wife was the property of her husband. Aristotle said that a woman was somewhere between a free man and a slave. In parts of India, widows were burned on their husbands' funeral pyres. Lauren, if you look at history, you'll find that Christian missionaries were a major influence in stopping such centuries-old practices and ideas."

"I have a question about that," said Brett. "Christians often talk about all the compassion they have for people, but what about all the founding fathers of America who professed to be Christians and owned slaves? How would you explain that?"

"In two minutes or in twelve hours?" asked Jamal.

Everyone laughed, which broke some of the natural tension of the discussion. Several of them went back to the counter for refills, and Jessica prayed silently for Andrea. Nick and Brett headed for the restroom. "How are you for time?" Nick asked.

"I'm still good," said Brett. "This is interesting, though it's all over the map. Your friends know their stuff. Hey, I meant to ask you when his name came up yesterday. Is Jamal . . ."

"From Notre Dame?" Nick cut in. Brett nodded. "He's the one. I'll tell you what—he's got an amazing story, too. I mean, unless you think testimonies are a waste of time." Nick smiled and Brett smacked his arm.

Seven

JESUS CHRIST AS A MAN OF HISTORY

BACK AT THE TABLE, Jamal picked up where they'd left off. "People are generally comfortable with what they're accustomed to. There have always been committed Christians living within and participating in broken social systems. I'm not proud of it and I won't deny it. Some of my ancestors were slaves here in America, so I've given serious thought to this. However, even more noteworthy than the Christians who owned slaves, whether in the United States or the New Testament era Roman Empire, is the fact that slavery was ended in great measure by Christian activists. For example, historians credit the British evangelical William Wilberforce as the primary force behind the ending of the international slave trade, just prior to the American Civil War. Two-thirds of the members of the American abolition society in 1835 were Christian ministers."

"I'm still holding that the teachings of Jesus have suppressed women, education, and science," said Andrea.

You would, thought Nick.

Lord, please affirm Your love for her, prayed Jessica. *For some reason she feels very strongly about this.*

Mina paused before responding. She didn't wish to be jumping all over Andrea's comments, yet they *were* largely ungrounded. "Do you know that all but one of the first 123 colleges in colonial America were originally Christian institutions? Many of the founders of modern science were Christians. Men like Kepler, Boyle, Pascal, Pasteur, Newton, and so forth. Not much suppression there."

"Hang on a second," said Nick, a bit too loudly. "Mina, regardless of things done in the name of Christ, good or bad, I think we need to get back to our original conversation about the identity of the true historical Christ. I was hoping you and Jamal could share some of the evidence you explained to me last year for Christ existing in history. I think we need to respond to the comments from Russell and Hitchens that Brett voiced early on. How can we know Christ even existed?"

"I agree," said Brett. "I would like some historical

evidence that Christ existed, especially apart from the Bible, which is certainly suspect if not corrupted."

"I'll be glad to provide some evidence apart from the Bible," said Jamal. "However, Brett, a bias against the accuracy of the twenty-seven individual New Testament books, just because they are 'in the Bible,' is historically unwarranted and unjustifiable. Even if you are skeptical toward Christianity, the Bible is a trustworthy historical document."[16]

Brett nodded and Jamal continued. "Even the American revolutionary Thomas Paine, who held Christianity in utter contempt, did not question the historicity of Jesus of Nazareth. While Paine believed that the biblical statements regarding Jesus' deity were mythological, he still held that Jesus actually lived. 'He (Jesus Christ) was a virtuous and amiable man. The morality that he preached and practiced was of the most benevolent kind; and though similar systems of morality had been preached by Confucius, and by some of the Greek philosophers, and by many good men in all ages, it has not been exceeded by any.'"[17]

"Listen to this quote I found last year while I was researching my research paper," said Nick. "It's from F. F. Bruce, Rylands Professor of Biblical Criticism and Exegesis at the University of Manchester. 'Some writers may toy with the fancy of a "Christ-myth," but they do not do so on the ground of historical evidence. The historicity of Christ is as axiomatic for an unbiased historian as the historicity of

Julius Caesar. It is not the historians who propagate the "Christ-myth" theories.'"[18]

"Okay," said Brett. "Show me the evidence!"

Jamal spoke up, "Brett, I brought some things I've been researching for a presentation I'll be giving in a couple weeks. They're on my computer, and if it's all right with you, I'll either read them or have you read them here at the table."

Brett nodded. Nick realized he was the type who wanted action. *Makes sense he rides that motorcycle,* he thought.

"Great. Let's begin with the secular authorities on Jesus' historicity. By secular, I mean non-Christian, non-Jewish, and generally hostile toward Christianity. First, there was Cornelius Tacitus (AD 55–120). He was a Roman historian who lived through the reigns of half a dozen emperors. He has been called the 'greatest historian' of ancient Rome, an individual generally acknowledged among scholars for his moral 'integrity and essential goodness.'"[19]

"Scott, is what Jamal is saying true?" asked Brett.

"Yes, it is," Scott replied. "Tacitus's most acclaimed works are the *Annals* and *Histories*. The *Annals* cover the period from Augustus's death in AD 14 to that of Nero in AD 68, while the *Histories* begin after Nero's death and proceeded to that of Domitian in AD 96."[20]

"Who would like to read from Tacitus?" asked Jamal.

"I will," said Jessica, finally speaking for the first time. At least *out loud.*

Jamal handed her his computer.

But not all the relief that could come from man, not all
the bounties that the prince could bestow, nor all the
atonements which could be presented to the gods, availed
to relieve Nero from the infamy of being believed to
have ordered the conflagration, the fire of Rome. Hence
to suppress the rumor, he falsely charged with the guilt,
and punished with the most exquisite tortures, the persons commonly called Christians, who were hated for
their enormities. Christus, the founder of the name, was
put to death by Pontius Pilate, procurator of Judea in
the reign of Tiberius: but the pernicious superstition,
repressed for a time, broke out again, not only through
Judea, where the mischief originated, but through the city
of Rome also.[21]

"Tacitus doesn't seem to like Christians," observed Jessica, "but he agrees with the creed we used to say in church
where Christ 'suffered under Pontius Pilate.'"

"Excellent observation, Jessica," said Jamal as he took
back his computer and started pulling up another historian. "At this point we are confirming that Christ was a
man of history, and even the most antagonistic historians
acknowledge multiple facts concerning Christ, such as His
dying. Lucian, a Greek satirist of the second century, spoke

scornfully toward Christ and the Christians, never assuming or arguing that they were unreal. Brett, will you read part of these two pages from Lucian's *The Death of Peregrine*?"

Brett reached for the computer and began to read.

The Christians, you know, worship a man to this day—the distinguished personage who introduced their novel rites, and was crucified.[22]

"Aha! This forthcoming part about their being 'misguided' sounds true," said Brett.

You see, these misguided creatures start with the general convictions that they are immortal for all time, which explains the contempt of death and voluntary self-devotion which are so common among them; and then it was impressed on them by their original lawgiver that they are all brothers, from the moment that they are converted and deny the gods of Greece, and worship the crucified sage, and live after his laws. All this they take quite on faith, with the result that they despise all worldly goods alike, regarding them merely as common property.[23]

"Brett," said Nick, "think about what you read. Lucian thought the followers of Christ were misguided, but he doesn't try to dispute the historical fact that Christ was cru-cified and that His followers were devoted in both their worship of Christ and kindness toward one another."

Jamal retrieved his computer and pulled up another one. "Suetonius, a Roman historian, court official under Hadrian, and annalist of the Imperial House, stated in his *Life of Claudius* 25.4, 'As the Jews were making constant disturbances at the instigation of Chrestus (another spelling of Christus), he (Claudius) expelled them from Rome.'[24] Luke refers to this event in Acts 18:2, which took place in AD 49. In another work, Suetonius wrote about the fire that swept through Rome in AD 64 under the reign of Nero. Suetonius writes that 'punishment by Nero was inflicted on the Christians, a class of men given to a new and mis-chievous superstition.'"[25]

"Wow, I didn't know that Suetonius had written that," said Scott. "I had read about Pliny the Younger writing of Christ, but this is interesting."

Andrea rolled her eyes and looked at Brett, who was seated to her left. Brett leaned toward her and whispered, "Who was Pliny the Younger?"

"Jamal, who was Pliny the Younger?" blurted Andrea.

Scott automatically looked to Jamal, then quickly avoided eye contact with him. He knew that Pliny had killed many Christians and didn't want to reopen the discussion about evils done by non-Christians.

"Andrea, Pliny was the Governor of Bithynia in Asia Minor in AD 112. Pliny was writing the emperor Trajan to seek counsel on how to treat the Christians. He explained that he had been killing all the Christians he encountered—men and women, boys and girls—but that there were so many being put to death he wondered if he should continue killing anyone who was discovered to be a Christian, or if he should kill only certain ones. He explained that he had made the Christians bow down to the statues of Trajan. Pliny goes on to say that he also 'made them curse Christ, which a genuine Christian cannot be induced to do.'[26]

"Let me read to you from the same letter in which Pliny is speaking of the Christians being tried. 'They affirmed, however, that the whole of their guilt, or their error, was that they were in the habit of meeting on a certain fixed day before it was light, when they sang in alternate verse a hymn to Christ as to a god, and bound themselves to a solemn oath, not to do any wicked deeds, but never commit any fraud, theft, adultery, never to falsify their word, not to deny a trust when they should be called upon to deliver it up.'"[27]

Eight

DO YOU
BELIEVE
ANYTHING
IN HISTORY?

"ARE THOSE ALL the sources you have?" Lauren asked.

"All the sources he has?" Scott glared back at her. "What do you mean by that? Do you believe *anything* in history? Why can't we just admit, as atheists or agnostics or whatevers, that Jesus Christ existed in history, died on a cross, and had devout, though perhaps ignorant, followers? Is that really a problem? When atheists like Russell, Hitchens, and all the 'bloggers-who'll-never-be-scholars' question Christ's historicity, I think it does us a disservice. It proves we've never even bothered to look into it."

"I'll be glad to share a few more examples, Lauren," suggested Jamal.

"Please do." Lauren glared back at Scott.

"One of the first secular writers to mention Christ was Thallus. Dated perhaps AD 52, Thallus 'wrote a history of the Eastern Mediterranean world from the Trojan War to his own time.'[28] Unfortunately, his writing now exists only in fragments that have been cited by other writers. One such writer is Julius Africanus, a Christian who penned his work around AD 221. One very interesting passage relates to a comment made by Thallus about the darkness that enveloped the land during the late afternoon hours when Jesus died on the cross. Julius Africanus, a third-century historian, mentioned Thallus. Andrea, would you mind reading this?"

"No thank you."

Jamal smiled at her, then read it himself.

Thallus, in the third book of his histories, explains away the darkness as an eclipse of the sun—unreasonably, as it seems to me (unreasonably, of course, because a solar eclipse could not take place at the time of the full moon, and it was at the season of the Paschal full moon that Christ died).[29]

"Why is this Africanus's reference to Thallus any big deal?" asked Brett.

"Well, it's important historically because it's another early, non-Christian reference to Jesus Christ. This specific reference shows that the gospel account of the darkness that fell upon the land during Christ's crucifixion was well known and required naturalistic explanations from non-Christians. Thallus did not doubt that Jesus had been crucified and that an unusual event had occurred in nature that required an explanation. What occupied his mind was the task of coming up with a different interpretation. The basic facts were not called into question."[30]

"Thanks for sharing all this," commented Brett. "I honestly didn't know there was so much documentation of Christ outside the New Testament. None of it proves He was God, of course, or even that He was good. The New Testament describes Him condemning people to hell, driving people from the temple with a whip, and even cursing a fig tree for not bearing fruit. He's not someone I'd want to follow, but you've given me reason to believe He existed in history."

"Those are reasonable objections," said Jamal, "and I'll be glad to deal with each one of them in further conversation. Hopefully, for right now, we've established some historical grounds that Christ did exist, and I would also like to take a minute to address your objection that we can't know if Jesus was *good*."

Brett looked at his watch. "Go ahead."

"Even some of the pagan writers of the first century saw Jesus as good. Let me read from one last non-Christian, non-Jewish first-century writer. In the later part of the first century, Mara Bar-Serapion, a Syrian and probably a Stoic philosopher, wrote a letter from prison to his son, encouraging him to pursue wisdom. In his letter he compares Jesus to the philosophers Socrates and Pythagoras. Nick?"

Nick took the computer and read with genuine interest.

What advantage did the Athenians gain from putting Socrates to death? Famine and plague came upon them as a judgment for their crime. What advantage did the men of Samos gain from burning Pythagoras? In a moment their land was covered with sand. What advantage did the Jews gain from executing their wise King? It was just after that their kingdom was abolished. God justly avenged these three wise men: the Athenians died of hunger; the Samians were overwhelmed by the sea; the Jews, ruined and driven from their land, live in complete dispersion. But Socrates did not die for good; he lived on in the teaching of Plato. Pythagoras did not die for good; he lived on in the statue of Hera. Nor did the wise King die for good; He lived on in the teaching which He had given.[31]

"What do you all observe from this?" Jamal asked.

Brett spoke up. "This writer seems to have a love for philosophers. The 'wise King' seems to describe Christ. Obviously, because of his reference to the dispersion of the Jews, this was written after AD 70 and the 'wise King' lived before AD 70. Clearly, Mara Bar-Serapion is not a Christian like you guys since he puts Jesus on equal footing with Socrates and Pythagoras."

"I agree with you, Brett," said Nick. "He also has Jesus living on through His teaching rather than His resurrection. But he thought Jesus a good enough person to warrant God's judgment on the Jews. And he certainly didn't question whether Christ really lived or not."

Andrea raised her voice. "So you've proved Jesus lived. What's the big deal? That doesn't make Him God. You can't prove He was born of a virgin, you can't prove His miracles, and you can't prove He rose from the dead. We spent all this time talking and we didn't learn a thing."

"Andrea, do you remember the time you stopped by my office last spring and I explained some of the evidence for Christ's miracles, and specifically His resurrection? I'll be glad to review some of that evidence with you if you'd like."

"Actually, I've got to go," said Brett. "I have to meet my girlfriend for dinner. But Jamal, I do appreciate you walking us through the historical evidence for Christ's existence. I'll make sure I'm at your lecture in a couple weeks!"

Jamal stood to shake Brett's hand and Andrea stood up too, saying, "You know, I'd better go as well." As they were all saying their good-byes, Andrea realized, for a fleeting moment, how persuasive and kind Jamal was in his defense of Christ's existence to Brett and his friends. Then Lauren giggled and said, "Oh my goodness, Jamal! How tall are you?"

Puh-leeze, Lauren! He hears that all the time, Andrea thought to herself. *Even my atheist friend is trying to flirt with Jamal.*

"I'm six feet six inches tall, which is pretty average in Texas! Look, why don't we all meet here again sometime? Also, I'd love for all of you to come out to the debate in three weeks."

"We already announced it at our atheist group," said Brett.

"Excellent. Well, it was a pleasure meeting you Brett, Scott, and Lauren. Andrea, thanks for hanging out."

Nine

JAMAL'S DEBATE

ANDREA HAD BEEN wrestling with her beliefs about Christ. She couldn't believe that both Nick and Jessica had fully devoted themselves to Jesus this past year. She didn't struggle so much with His virgin birth, deity, or resurrection. It was just so hard to believe He was the only way to salvation. What about all those children who die without hearing the gospel? It seemed so wrong to think of them in hell because they never knew about Jesus.

She had turned to the atheist club thinking they would be intellectually honest, but they had their struggles and inconsistencies too. More recently her favorite professor, Dr. William Peterson, had retired from full-time teaching and now seemed more open to Christianity. She was curious about his response to Jamal's views and hoped he would ask Jamal some good questions at tonight's forum with Drs. Hitzfield and Gouffran.

Andrea was running late and couldn't find parking anywhere close to Wesley Auditorium. By the time she finally arrived—forty-five minutes into the program—she found every seat taken. "Unbelievable," she muttered. From where she stood in the back she could see Nick, Mina, and Jessica seated in the front row, and her friends Brett, Lauren, and Scott right behind them. She rolled her eyes.

On stage, Dr. Peterson was shaking hands with one of the presenters and taking the microphone. "Thank you, Dr. Hitzfield. I'd now like to invite Mr. Jamal Washington to the lectern. Mr. Washington, you have fifteen minutes to respond to Dr. Hitzfield's argument against the historical reliability of the testimony about Christ."

Jamal stepped up to the microphone wearing a black suit and stylish glasses. With his athletic build and scholarly bearing, he brought natural authority to the platform. *No wonder my friends all flirt with him*, thought Andrea.

After a few introductory remarks and greetings, Jamal dove right in. "Dr. Hitzfield, we can't neglect the historical fact that you admitted to about the persecution of the early Christians for their public reports that Jesus had lived, died, rose from the dead, and appeared to many after His resurrection. These early Christians had nothing to gain and everything to lose for their testimony that these things had actually happened. For this reason their accounts are highly significant historical sources."

Jamal then turned to the audience. "Pay close attention to what I am about to say. This is an argument you don't want to miss. Recorded in the pages of the New Testament, biblical scholars have identified what they believe are at least portions of early Christian creedal confessions that were formulated and passed on verbally years before they were recorded in the books of the New Testament. As Dr. Gary Habermas explains, these affirmations 'preserve some of the earliest reports concerning Jesus from about AD 30–50. Therefore, in a real sense, the creeds preserve pre-New Testament material, and are our earliest sources for the life of Jesus.'[32] In other words, these sayings were memorized and passed down orally."

Jamal flipped the page of his notebook and only briefly looked down. "Examples of these creedal affirmations embedded in the New Testament and identified by leading scholars from Oxford, Cambridge, and Princeton would include Luke 24:34, Romans 1:3–4, Romans 4:24–25, Romans 10:9–10, 1 Timothy 3:16, Philippians 2:6–11, 2 Timothy 2:8, 1 Peter 3:18, 1 John 4:2, and 1 Corinthians 11:23–26."

Jamal continued, "Ninety percent of all scholars who have published on the resurrection in the last thirty years, including the most liberal scholars at Ivy League institutions, admit the early dating of 1 Corinthians, between AD 53 and 57, and they also acknowledge that the apostle Paul is the real author. Dr. Gary Habermas, who earned his PhD from Michigan State, pointed out that when Paul speaks of the Lord's Supper in 1 Corinthians,[33] he presents a fixed tradition that is probably based on material independent of the sources for the synoptic gospels. Jeremias notes that Paul's words *received* and *delivered* are not Paul's typical terms, but 'represent the rabbinical technical terms' for passing on tradition. In fact, Jeremias asserts that this material was formulated 'in the very earliest period; at any rate before Paul . . . a pre-Pauline formula.' Paul is actually pointing out that 'the chain of tradition goes back unbroken to Jesus himself.'[34]

"From just a historical perspective, scholars know that Paul is using pre-existing material, some of which are called 'creedal confessions' that pre-date the writing of his letter. Now, let's turn our attention to one of the creedal confessions in 1 Corinthians. 'For I delivered to you as of first importance what I also received, that Christ died for our sins according to the Scriptures, and that He was buried, and that He was raised on the third day according to the Scriptures, and that He appeared to Cephas, then to the twelve.'"[35]

Jamal looked up at Dr. Peterson and then back to Drs. Hitzfield and Gouffran before continuing. "The evidence that suggests this material existed before Paul's conversion is clinched in verse 11, where Paul remarks that he has stated what was the common proclamation of the apostles. 'Whether then it was I or they, so we preach and so you believed.'[36]

"Ladies and gentlemen, the narrative of this piece, along with the book of Mark that I mentioned in my opening remarks, lacks the legendary embellishment of the miracles recorded by Homer and the other ancient poets. After citing the creed, Paul goes on to reference specific names of eyewitnesses—including James, the brother of Christ, who wasn't a believer until *after* he had seen the resurrected Christ. Why was James converted? *Because of what he saw.* Then Paul adds that Christ appeared to over 500 of the brethren, 'Most of them are alive, though some have fallen asleep.' Now, don't miss this. Paul gives the creed, defends it, talks about eyewitness accounts, and then reminds them that most of the eyewitnesses are still alive. What is he doing here? He is putting his entire reputation on the line by saying, 'If you don't believe me, check it out with the 500 eyewitnesses. They will tell you they saw the resurrected Christ.' Take note of this. Paul wasn't calling his followers to a blind faith, but to a faith based on a historical event—the resurrection of Christ.

"And now my time is up."

Dr. William Peterson was silent as he listened to Jamal. As the moderator, he was determined not to reveal any emotion, but in his heart, he felt pleased with Jamal's lecture. Dr. Peterson had rejected the resurrection for over thirty-five years, but privately he had recently become persuaded of its foundational truth. The early data Jamal cited had awakened his convictions several months earlier, and his own research affirmed that the resurrection of Christ could not be explained away. All the false claims of 'Christ never died on the cross,' 'the disciples had hallucinations,' 'the disciples stole the body,' and 'Christ was never buried' failed to convince him intellectually. The only person who was aware of Dr. Peterson's recent conversion was his wife, Susan. He also planned to share it with his students when the time was right, for he felt ashamed in his heart for deceiving so many impressionable students over the years and turning them away from Christ.

Ten

ATHEISM, DAVID HUME, AND THE DENIAL OF MIRACLES

DR. PETERSON TOOK the microphone. "Thank you, Mr. Washington. Now, Dr. Franck Gouffran, you have fifteen minutes to give a rebuttal to Jamal Washington's original defense of the resurrection."

Gouffran jumped right in. "Jamal, perhaps the literature you cited does provide very early attestation that people were claiming to have seen a risen Christ. I'll give you that argument and consent, but it won't convince me as an educated man that the resurrection actually did happen. What I would like to propose is that, regardless of the miraculous claims of Christ and His followers, along with the evidence you provided, it is unreasonable—irrational, actually—to believe that God exists, that Jesus is God, and that He was raised from the dead.

"Now, I would like to go to the argument of noted philosopher David Hume. This argument has not been adequately rebutted by any Christian that I know of. I'll read from David Hume and then share a few comments:

> A miracle is a violation of the laws of nature; and as a firm and unalterable experience has established these laws, the proof against a miracle, from the very nature of the fact, is as entire as any argument from experience can possibly be imagined. . . . Nothing is esteemed a miracle, if it ever happened in the common course of nature. It is no miracle that a man, seemingly in good health, should die on a sudden: because such a kind of death, though more unusual than any other, has yet been frequently observed to happen. But it is a miracle that a dead man should come to life; because that has never been observed in any age or country. There must, therefore, be a uniform experience against every miraculous event, otherwise the event would not merit the appellation. And as a uniform experience amounts to a proof, there is here a direct and full proof be destroyed, or the miracle rendered credible, but by an opposite proof, which is superior.[37]

"Faculty, students, and guests, what Hume has brilliantly revealed is that the one who believes in God must believe in a natural order since without such an order, there cannot be any way of recognizing exceptions to the order. Then, Hume clearly reminds the Christian that the probability for the Christian's alleged violations of natural laws must always be much less than the probability that the exception has occurred.[38]

"Dr. Peterson and Mr. Washington, let me summarize Hume's argument for the audience:

1. A miracle is by definition a rare occurrence.
2. Natural law is by definition a description of regular occurrence.
3. The evidence for the regular is always greater than that for the rare.
4. Wise individuals always base belief on the greater evidence.
5. Therefore, wise individuals should never believe in miracles.[39]

"Perhaps those of you who are Christians would respond, 'Even if Hume's philosophical argument against miracles is good, *we have faith* that Jesus is God!' If a Christian chooses to believe in virgin births, talking snakes, or a resurrection of Jesus, it seems that the only basis for such a belief is 'faith.' But let me make it perfectly clear. Blind faith is *not knowledge*. Though one might claim to be truthful in exercising blind faith, it is not *intellectually* honest.

"The religious philosopher William James once gave a lecture entitled, 'The Will to Believe.' He seems to have influenced many churchgoing Christians, especially here in the South where there appears to be a mega-church on every corner. James thought it was acceptable for Christians to violate the principle of evidence as long as their faith was at work. In other words, a Christian may not have knowledge or evidence of truth, but so long as he has *faith* in God, and his family seems happy, his marriage is better, and his relationships seem 'authentic,' having *faith* is just fine.

"I would argue that the blind faith of William James is illogical, and that there is no need for this blind faith. If Christians wish to be authentic, they must believe that which is rational, trust their senses and science, and deny these acts called miracles. Thank you very much."

Eleven

THE POSSIBILITY OF MIRACLES

DR. PETERSON RETURNED to the podium. "Now Instructor Washington will have fifteen minutes to respond to Dr. Franck Gouffran."

Jamal began, "Dr. Gouffran, numerous Christian philosophers have rebutted Hume. Let me adapt from Dr. Norman Geisler, who earned his PhD in philosophy at Loyola. He pointed out that when Hume speaks of 'uniform' experience in his argument, his notion either begs the question or else is special pleading. It begs the question if Hume presumes in advance of looking at the evidence. For how can we know that all possible experience will confirm naturalism, unless we have access to all possible experiences, past, present, and future? If, on the other hand, Hume simply means by 'uniform' experience the select experiences of *some* persons who have *not* encountered a miracle, then this is special pleading."[40]

Jamal continued, "Dr. Geisler also writes that Hume does not really *weigh* the evidence for miracles; rather he *adds* evidence against them. Since death occurs over and over again and resurrection occurs only on rare occasions at best, Hume simply adds up all the deaths against the very few alleged resurrections and rejects the latter. But this does not involve weighing evidence to determine whether or not that person, say Jesus of Nazareth, has been raised from the dead. It is simply adding up the evidence of all other occasions where people have *not* been raised and using it to overwhelm any possible evidence that some person who died was brought back to life.

"Furthermore, his argument also equates quantity of evidence and probability. It says, in effect, that we should always believe what is most probable (in the sense of 'enjoying the highest odds'). But this is silly. On this basis, a wise person would never believe that a golfer has hit a hole in one since the odds are against it. What Hume seems to overlook is that wise people base their beliefs on facts, not simply odds. Sometimes the 'odds' against an event are high, based on past observation, but the *evidence* for the event is very good, based on current observation or reliable testimony.

Dr. Gouffran, David Hume's argument confuses *quantity* of evidence with the *quality* of evidence. Evidence should be *weighed*, not *added*."[41]

Jamal smiled and looked at Dr. Peterson and some of the faculty in the front row. "Come to think of it, when Dr. Peterson and I were golfing with Dr. Chase Heindrich last spring, Dr. Heindrich hit a hole in one! Can you believe that?"

"No!" shouted two of Dr. Heindrich's colleagues from the front row. The audience laughed as various ones pointed out Dr. Chase Heindrich in the front row, and one student yelled, "Go, Dr. Chase!"

Jamal continued, "Believe me, Dr. Gouffran, if you knew Dr. Heindrich's golfing ability, you would be a skeptic too. But there were two eyewitnesses, and despite Dr. Heindrich's past golfing experience, Dr. Peterson and I know that he, in fact, hit a hole in one. Now, getting back to Hume, he confuses the probability of historical events with the way in which scientists employ probability to formulate scientific law. Let me read something from Dr. Ronald Nash, who earned his PhD at Syracuse.

Critics of Hume have complained that his argument is based on a defective view of probability. For one thing, Hume treats the probability of events in history like miracles in the same way he treats the probability of recurring events that give rise to the formulation of scientific laws. In the case of scientific laws, probability is tied to the frequency of occurrence; the more times scientists observe similar occurrences under similar conditions, the greater the probability that their formulation of the law is correct. But historical events including miracles are different; the events of the history are unique and non-repeatable. Therefore, treating historical events, including miracles, with the same notion of probability the scientist uses in formulating his laws ignores a fundamental difference between the two subject matters.[42]

"Lastly, regarding your reference to *The Will to Believe*, by William James, I would argue that it actually takes more will to *not* believe. The historically verifiable early documentation that I provided for the death of Christ in the creedal language of 1 Corinthians 15 and Mark, the lack of legendary embellishment, and numerous accounts of eyewitnesses must be dealt with. In addition, one must come to terms with the transformed lives of the apostles.

"By failing to contend with the historical evidence of Christ's resurrection and the possibility of miracles, you have avoided the historical evidence for Christ's resurrection and have 'willed to believe' a denial of miracles."

Jamal paused to read some notes that he had taken during Dr. Gouffran's lecture. "At the beginning of your rebuttal,

Dr. Gouffran, you stated, 'Perhaps the literature you cited does provide very early attestation that people were claiming to have seen a risen Christ. I'll give you that argument and consent, but it won't convince me as an educated man that the resurrection actually did happen.' You then added, 'What I would like to propose is that, regardless of the miraculous claims of Christ and His followers, along with the evidence you provided, it is unreasonable to believe that God exists, that Jesus is God, and that He was raised from the dead.' Your remarks appear to indicate a bias of anti-supernaturalism rather than a willingness to carefully investigate the evidence. This is not an open-minded historical examination of the evidence, but a 'will to believe' that there is no God, no miracles, and no resurrection. Thank you for your time."

As Jamal returned to his seat, the audience broke out in applause.

Andrea glanced at Lauren, Scott, and Brett. They were not clapping. Though she did not wish to admit it, Andrea felt that Jamal's arguments had refuted the rhetoric of his two opponents. For just a second, she considered whether what he was saying was true.

Dr. Peterson, maintaining his neutrality as moderator, quieted the audience and took additional questions from the panel of professors and several students in the audience. He too was considering the evidence for the historical resurrection. He then thanked the presenters, announced the next event in the series, and thanked everyone for attending.

Afterwards, Mina and Jessica spotted Andrea at the back and made their way to her. "Andrea, so good to see you!" exclaimed Mina. She threw her arms around her in a big hug like old times. Though Andrea tried to act cold and standoffish, she found herself fighting a smile. She was glad that Mina and Jessica were there.

Meanwhile, Nick walked over to Scott, Lauren, and Brett. "Hey, Nick," said Brett. "I may not agree with Jamal, but I'll admit he definitely won that debate."

"No, he didn't," said Lauren.

Brett just looked at her. "I disagree, Lauren. Jamal made Franck Gouffran look like the one avoiding evidence and 'willing to believe.'"

Lauren looked at Scott. "Who do you think won?"

"Well, I have always liked Dr. Jurgen Hitzfield, but Jamal's defense of Paul's usage of early creedal language and eyewitness accounts of the resurrection was pretty convincing from a historical perspective. I'm not sure how to deal with it, honestly, but I still have questions about Old Testament ethics and the problem of evil. Jamal might have won the debate, but I'm staying agnostic."

Nick looked at Scott. "I thought you were an atheist, not an agnostic."

"I'm both," said Scott, grinning as he looked away.

Twelve

A NEW CHAPTER FOR THE PETERSONS

"SWEETHEART, you did an exceptional job moderating the debate," said Susan Peterson.

"Thank you, Susan," responded the professor as he took off his jacket and tie.

"Did you tell Jamal or Nick about your new faith?" asked Susan as she handed Dr. Peterson a small bowl of Blue Bunny ice cream.

"No, not yet. I haven't told anyone but you."

"Why not?"

Dr. Peterson didn't answer.

"You haven't told anyone but me? It's been over a month since you prayed to receive Christ."

"Well, it just wasn't the right time. I wanted to tell Pastor Greg this Sunday, but he seemed busy and I just didn't have a good opportunity."

"Bill, I hope you are not afraid of a backlash. I think at some point soon it would be good to tell your friends. You know Jamal and Nick will be excited, and even though some of your colleagues might give you a hard time, they will still respect you. Even more importantly, God will honor you. Remember the teaching of Christ, 'Whoever acknowledges me before men, I will also acknowledge him before my Father in heaven. But whoever disowns me before men, I will disown him before my Father in heaven.'[43] Bill, you've taught a false view of Christ for so long, I think you should start telling everyone about your conversion and humbly admit you were wrong in some of your teaching. Why not start proclaiming the true historic Christ?"

"Susan, you're absolutely right." Dr. Peterson paused to scoop them both more ice cream, then continued. "I didn't want the word to get out before tonight. As the moderator, I didn't want the attention shifted toward me. I also didn't want the audience to think I was biased, but I figured that at the right time I would share my change of thinking about Christ to all the faculty and students. In fact, I have been seriously thinking about reserving Wesley Auditorium so that I can lecture on "Did Jesus Claim to be God?" I am unashamed of the gospel of Jesus Christ and believe this would provide a good opportunity to present my case for Him."

Susan threw her arms around her husband. "I believe in you, honey. God will use your testimony."

"I know the critics will come after me, but that's what I deserve for being so stubborn and deceiving so many young minds over the years. May God have mercy on me."

"Bill, if God could use Saul of Tarsus, who persecuted the Christian church, to write large portions of the New Testament, I'm confident He will give you wisdom to influence Opal University."

Thirteen

NICK
AND
JESSICA

JESSICA GRABBED her phone. "Hello?"

"Hey Jess, it's me. Nick."

"Hi, Nick."

"I know back in the summer you told me you didn't want to go out on dates with me, but I was wondering if you would change your mind long enough for me to take you to dinner on Friday?"

"Um, okay. Sure! That sounds fun."

"Great! I was thinking we could go to Fort Worth, eat Mexican, and then go two-stepping at Billy Bob's. Zac Brown Band is playing outside and I have two tickets. Does that sound like fun?"

"Oh yeah! That sounds great!"

Three nights later, as Nick and Jessica were driving from Dallas to Fort Worth, Nick asked Jessica, "How did the discussion with the girls go after the *I am Second* Bible study last night?"

"It went pretty well, but when I went to read a passage from the Bible, one girl spoke up and said, 'I don't like to discuss religion, especially Jesus.' My initial response was, 'Okay, then why did you come to a Bible study?' She said she was an avid fan of Anne Rice, the vampire novelist, and heard we were featuring her film. I asked what she thought about the film, and she didn't have much to say. Nick, do you remember last year when we were dating, before I trusted Jesus, I would always try to change the topic when you brought Him up? Will you please forgive me for that?"

"Jessica, I've already forgiven you. We've already talked about this."

"Thanks. You know, the very name of Jesus seems to bother people. It makes them uncomfortable, or angry, or both. So many of the girls try to change the subject when He comes up. It seems like you can talk about Buddha, Muhammad, or Confucius all day and people don't get upset, but mention Jesus and it's all over. Why don't the others offend people the way Jesus does?"

Nick thought about that for a minute. "I think the reason is that those other religious leaders didn't claim to be God. That's the big difference between Jesus and the others. Jesus made astounding claims about Himself and it became clear that those claims identified Him as more than a prophet and teacher. Speaking of all this, did you hear the news from Dr. Peterson?"

"What news?"

"He became a Christian."

"What?!" Jessica couldn't believe what she was hearing. She had been praying for him almost every day.

"Yeah, he actually came to faith in Christ about a month ago."

"Nick, are you kidding me? That is so exciting!" Jessica started tearing up. "I had no idea."

"I assumed you already knew, Jess! He sent out the email this morning and announced his conversion. He's going to give a special lecture in three weeks on the deity of Christ. I can't believe you haven't heard. Every religion student was talking about it today."

"Have you talked to him?"

"No, not yet. I stopped by his office, but his secretary said he and Jamal were taking the day off to golf. I haven't talked with either one of them."

"That is such an answer to prayer! I'll bet your boldness in sharing the gospel with him that night we were at his house had an influence on him."

"I doubt that! All I remember from that night was feeling sorry for preaching at him. I think Jamal probably had more of an influence, but I'm just thankful that Dr. Peterson came to Christ. It's ultimately the Holy Spirit who pursues a relationship with us."

"Well, it's true that only God saves, but God definitely used you to bring me to faith."

Nick smiled and reached over to squeeze Jessica's hand. "And you certainly have changed."

"So have *you*." Jessica laughed.

"Yup. Before you became a Christian, Jess, you were one rude, stuck up . . ."

"Hey!" Jessica slapped Nick's arm. "Look at your goofy smile, Nick! I take back what I said—you haven't changed a bit!"

"Seriously, Jess," Nick continued, "God is doing great things through you. You have so much compassion in your humanitarian work with those children, you're leading girls to Christ, and volunteering at the shelter. You're like a beautiful version of Mother Teresa!"

"Flattery will get you nowhere!" Jessica squeezed Nick's arm.

"Then again, though you have some good qualities, I'm just not sure you'll be able to keep up with me on the two-step tonight," said Nick. They both laughed. Nick was a terrible dancer.

Fourteen

THE DEITY OF CHRIST IN THE BOOK OF MARK

ON MONDAY MORNING, all the students in Jamal's Introduction to the New Testament class were eager to talk about William Peterson's conversion and upcoming lecture. Jamal spent only a few minutes on the topic and then dove into his lecture.

"It is absolutely foolish when critics say the deity of Christ is not affirmed in the book of Mark, since Mark is the oldest of the four gospels. In chapter two, we see Jesus do something that only God can do; He forgives sins. Let me read it to you. 'Seeing their faith, Jesus said to the paralyzed man, "My child, your sins are forgiven."'"[44]

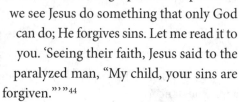

Jamal paused. "I know what some of you might be thinking, *That's no big deal. He's not claiming to be God.* But watch closely. According to Jewish theology, only God could say such a thing; the forgiveness of sin was the prerogative of God alone.[45] When the scribes heard Jesus forgiving the man's sins they were indignant. 'What is he saying? This is blasphemy! Only God can forgive sins!'[46]

"Class, do you see what is happening? When the religious leaders heard Him forgive sins, they accused Him of blasphemy. Look at this next slide. Dr. Lewis Sperry Chafer, founder and first president of Dallas Theological Seminary, wrote:"

> None on earth has either authority or right to forgive sin. None could forgive sin save the One against whom all have sinned. When Christ forgives sin, as he certainly did, he was not exercising a human prerogative. Since none but God can forgive sins, it is conclusively demonstrated that Christ, since he forgave sins, is God.[47]

Nick's hand shot up.

"Yes, Nick?"

"Okay, I am convinced of Christ's claims of deity in the book of John, like when He calls Himself, 'I AM,' the name

God revealed to Moses. But I'm not too convinced of this one in Mark. It seems that this reference you provided is a bit of a stretch. I can forgive people without claiming to be God. People do it all the time. Even when I considered myself an agnostic I forgave people."

"Ah, Nick! Yes, one can say, 'I forgive you,' but only if he is the one who has been sinned against. Nick, let's say you sin against me. We're out on the court and I keep blocking your shots, so you shout some defamatory language at me in the heat of the moment. I have the right to forgive you. But if you sin against someone else, let's say your older brother, I have no such right. The paralytic in Mark 2 had not sinned against the man Jesus. The two men had never seen each other before. The paralytic had sinned against God. When Jesus came along and, under His own authority, said, 'Your sins are forgiven,' He was speaking as God. We can forgive sins committed against us, but in no way can anyone forgive sins committed against God . . . unless he's God."

Jamal continued, "It's no wonder the Jews reacted so violently when a carpenter from Nazareth made such a bold claim. This assertion that He could forgive sins was a startling exercise of a prerogative that belongs only to God.

"Yes, Emily?"

"That reference seems pretty unique. Are there any other references of Christ making bold claims in Mark's gospel?"

"Absolutely. Emily, why don't you read to us from the

book of Daniel, chapter seven, verses thirteen and fourteen. I want to talk about the phrase *Son of Man*."

As Emily found the passage and began reading, Jamal pulled the verses up on the screen so the whole class could see:

> In my vision at night I looked, and there before me was one like a son of man, coming with the clouds of heaven. He approached the Ancient of Days and was led into his presence. He was given authority, glory and sovereign power; all peoples, nations and men of every language worshiped him. His dominion is an everlasting dominion that will not pass away, and his kingdom is one that will never be destroyed. (Daniel 7:13–14)

"Thank you, Emily. Now, Scripture is clear that only God is to be worshiped. Yes, Emily?"

"Where does Scripture say that only God should be worshipped? Didn't Jesus receive worship?"

"Yes He did, and the very fact that He received worship confirmed His deity. As for a reference, Jesus tells Satan in Matthew 4:10, 'You must worship the Lord your God and serve only him.' He's actually quoting from Deuteronomy 6:13, an Old Testament passage very familiar to the Jews."[48]

"Now, back to the *Son of Man* that Emily read about in

Daniel. Scripture is clear that only God is to be worshiped. However, Daniel sees a vision of this 'Son of Man' receiving worship. Now, take note that Daniel is speaking of a man that will be worshiped, even though the Scriptures had spoken about worshiping only God. Despite the common misperception, the term 'Son of Man' was not a reference to the *humanity* of Jesus, but to His *divinity*. Let me cite two scholarly writers, Komoszewski and Bowman, who explain Daniel's vision:

> In Daniel's vision, the humanlike figure possesses all judgment authority and rules over an everlasting kingdom. The notion of frailty and dependence is absent. The description of the figure as coming with the clouds also identifies him as divine, since elsewhere in the Old Testament the imagery of coming on clouds is used exclusively for divine figures.[49]

"We see Jesus referencing this particular passage in Mark 14. Let's take a look at that. Nick, would you read for us Mark 14:60–64?"

Nick opened his New Testament and began reading:

> Then the high priest stood up before them and asked Jesus, "Are you not going to answer? What is this testimony that these men are bringing against you?" But

Jesus remained silent and gave no answer. Again the high priest asked him, "Are you the Christ, the Son of the Blessed One?"

"I am," said Jesus. "And you will see the *Son of Man* sitting at the right hand of the Mighty One and coming on the clouds of heaven."

The high priest tore his clothes. "Why do we need any more witnesses?" he asked. "You have heard the blasphemy. What do you think?"

They all condemned him as worthy of death.[50]

Jamal asked, "Why did they condemn Him as worthy of death?"

"Jesus was claiming to be God," said a student named John from the back row.

Jamal smiled. "Yes. The religious leaders knew Jesus' allusion and interpretation of Daniel 7:13. Jesus was claiming to be a divine, a heavenly figure who would sit at God's right hand, exercising supreme authority over all people for all eternity. No wonder the Jewish authorities were so upset—Jesus had committed blasphemy by claiming to be God! Clearly, Jesus had a divine self-consciousness.[51]

"Yes, John?" Jamal asked.

"Do we need to know this for our quiz?"

"Bad question. You have to know *everything* I say for the quiz," responded Jamal with a smile.

While several students began writing furiously, Jamal brought up a new PowerPoint slide. "So, an analysis of Christ's own testimony—which you might want to remember for the next quiz—shows He clearly claimed to be:"

> 1. The Son of the blessed God.
> 2. The One who would sit at the right hand of power.
> 3. The *Son of Man,* who would come on the clouds of heaven.

Jamal continued, "Each of these affirmations is distinctly messianic. The cumulative effect of all three is significant. The Sanhedrin, the Jewish court, caught all three points, and the high priest responded by tearing his garments and saying, 'Why do we need any more witnesses?'[52] They had finally heard it for themselves from Jesus' own mouth. He was convicted by His own words.[53]

"The next slide reveals the conclusion from Sir Robert Anderson, who was once head of criminal investigation at Scotland Yard. Here is what he observed:"

> No confirmatory evidence is more convincing than that of hostile witnesses, and the fact that the Lord laid claim to Deity is incontestably estab-

lished by the action of His enemies. We must remember that the Jews were not a tribe of ignorant savages, but a highly cultured and intensely religious people; and it was upon this very charge that, without a dissenting voice, His death was decreed by the Sanhedrin—their great national Council, composed of the most eminent of their religious leaders, including men of the type of Gamaliel, the first century Jewish philosopher and his famous pupil, Saul of Tarsus.[54]

"So Jesus clearly wanted to bear this testimony and claim to be God in front of the Sanhedrin?" Emily asked.

"Absolutely," said Jamal. "This is the testimony Jesus wanted to bear about Himself. We also see that the Jews understood His reply was His claim to be God. At this point they are faced with two alternatives. Either His assertions were outlandish blasphemy, or He was God. His judges saw the issue clearly—so clearly that they crucified Him and taunted Him on the cross saying, 'He trusts in God. Let God rescue him now if he wants him, for he said, "I am the Son of God."'"[55]

"What's the deal with the high priest tearing his garment?" Nick asked.

"It was a custom of Jewish law that revealed horror because of blasphemy spoken. I have an observation on that question from H. B. Swete, former Regius professor of divinity at Cambridge University. Dr. Swete wrote:

> The law forbade the High Priest to rend his garment in private troubles (Leviticus 10:6; 21:10), but when acting as judge, he was required by custom to express in this way his horror of any blasphemy uttered in his presence. The relief of the embarrassed judge is manifest. If trustworthy evidence is not forthcoming, the necessity for it had now been superseded: the Prisoner had incriminated himself.[56]

"While we're on this topic, I have an interesting piece on the trial of Jesus from the perspective of a lawyer, Irwin Linton. This was no ordinary trial." Jamal flipped through his slides for a moment, and then said, "Take a look at this:

Unique among criminal trials is this one in which not the actions but the identity of the accused is this issue. The criminal charge laid against Christ, the confession or testimony or, rather, act in presence of the court, on which He was convicted, the interrogation by the Roman governor and the inscription and proclamation on His cross at the time of execution are all concerned with the one question of Christ's real identity and dignity. "What think ye of Christ? Whose son is he?"[57]

"Go ahead, Emily."

"I've heard from several people in the religious department that Dr. Peterson became a Christian and is convinced of the deity of Christ. Is that true?"

"Yes, it's true. But Dr. Peterson wants to personally break the news, so he is giving a special lecture in three weeks on the deity of Christ. He discussed it with me while we were golfing last week, and he is really hoping everyone will be there."

"Can we get extra credit?" blurted John, smiling.

Jamal just looked at John with a straight face and said nothing. After contemplating for a few seconds, Jamal said, "Tell you what. If any of you attend the lecture and write a two page analysis and critique of Dr. Peterson's lecture, I'll give you an extra credit quiz grade."

"Yes!" yelled John, pumping his fist in the air.

Jamal ignored him and continued, "Class, let me summarize some observations and share one more passage before I dismiss you." He looked around the room for a few moments, intentionally seeking eye contact. "In most trials the accused are tried for what they are alleged to have done, but this was not the case in the trial of Jesus. He was tried for what He *claimed to be*."

He paused, then continued. "The trial of Jesus should be sufficient to demonstrate *convincingly* that He confessed to His divinity. His judges attest to that claim, and on the day of Christ's crucifixion, His enemies acknowledged that He claimed to be God come in flesh. Pull out your Bibles and let's turn to Matthew 27. John, in a clear, loud voice, please read verses 41–43 for us."

As John found his place, Jamal put the passage up on the screen for those who didn't bring their Bibles.

> The leading priests, the teachers of religious law, and the elders also mocked Jesus. "He saved others," they scoffed, "but he can't save himself! So he is the King of Israel, is he? Let him come down from the cross right now, and we will believe in him! He trusted God, so let God rescue him now if he wants him! For he said, 'I am the Son of God.'"[58]

"Thanks for reading, John. See you next class."

Fifteen

WHAT DID OTHERS SAY ABOUT JESUS?

ON WEDNESDAY NIGHT, Brett, Scott, and Lauren again joined the group gathered at the Caruth Haven Coffeehouse to discuss the identity of Christ. Jamal kicked the evening off by presenting a concise case for the reliability of the New Testament, and Mina mentioned something related to Dr. Peterson's conversion. Scott followed with a comment that triggered some intense conversation.

"Jesus isn't even called God in the Bible."

Brett also chimed in. "He's right. I read the entire New Testament this summer and never found one verse."

Nick smiled. He'd heard Jamal teach on this.

Jamal took the cue. "You make a good observation, Scott. The explanation has to do with His name. What many people don't realize is that the words *Jesus Christ* are not a first and last name. They are a name and a *title*. The name 'Jesus' is derived from the Greek form of the name *Jeshua*, or Joshua, meaning 'Jehovah-Savior' or 'the Lord saves.' The title 'Christ' is derived from the Greek word for Messiah and means 'anointed one.' Two offices, king and priest, are indicated in the use of the title 'Christ'. The title affirms Jesus as the promised priest and king of Old Testament prophecies. This affirmation is crucial to a proper understanding about Jesus and Christianity."[59]

Jamal continued, "Brett, I would say that the New Testament clearly presents Christ as God. Most of the names applied to Christ are such that they could properly be applied only to one who was God. For example, Jesus is called God in the statement, 'Looking for that blessed hope, and the glorious appearing of the great God and our Saviour Jesus Christ.'"[60]

"Where is that verse?" asked Brett.

"Titus 2:13. But there are many others: John 1:1, Romans 9:5, Hebrews 1:8, 1 John 5:20–21."

"But didn't Jesus Himself quote from Psalms saying, 'You are gods'? Jesus certainly isn't described in the same way as God in the New Testament."

Jamal flipped open his laptop and pulled up his lecture notes. "What's your email address, Brett? I want to send you this document."

After sending the email to Brett, Jamal handed his computer to Jessica, who had been quiet all evening. "Jessica, why don't you read some of these Scripture references that attribute characteristics to Jesus that can be true only of God."

"Okay," said Jessica. "In Scripture, Jesus Christ is presented as:"

- Self-existent (see John 1:2; 8:58; 17:5; 17:24)
- Omnipresent (see Matthew 18:20; 28:20)
- Omniscient (see Matthew 17:22–27; John 4:16–18; 6:64)
- Omnipotent (see Matthew 8:26–27; Luke 4:38–41; 7:14–15; 8:24–25; Revelation 1:8)
- Possessing Eternal Life (see 1 John 5:11–12, 20)

Nick jumped in. "Another evidence that Jesus presented Himself as God was that He received honor and worship that only God should receive. This came up in our class the other day. In a confrontation with Satan, Jesus said, 'For the Scriptures say, "You must worship the Lord your God and serve only him."'"[61]

Andrea spoke up, "Okay, where are those references?"

"We read it in class the other day. It's from Matthew,

when Jesus was being tempted by Satan," responded Nick. "Hang on, I'll find it. Jamal do you know where that's from?"

"You're right, Nick. It's Matthew 4:10. Jesus also received worship as God in Matthew 14:33 and Matthew 28:9, and He claimed to be worthy of worship as God in John 5:23. In Hebrews 1:6 and Revelation 5:8–14 He is again the object of worship."

Scott interrupted, "But the Jews were devoutly mono-theistic and it seems that only non-Jews believed in Jesus as God through Paul's teaching."

Mina responded, "It is correct that the Jews were devoutly monotheistic, yet Jesus was a Jew, Paul was a Jew, and many of Christ's early followers were Jews. The verses that Jamal and Jessica referenced clearly reveal that they recognized Christ as God Himself."

"I'm still not sure about that, Mina," said Andrea.

"Okay, tell you what. How many Bibles do we have?" asked Jamal.

"It looks like five," said Jessica. She noticed that Brett and Andrea each brought a Bible.

"Andrea, do you have the Bible on your Mac?" asked Jamal.

"Yeah!"

"Will you look up Matthew 16:16? This comes after Jesus asked His disciples who they thought He was."

"Simon Peter answered, 'You are the Christ, the Son of

the living God.'" Andrea flushed as she read this. For some reason she felt nervous and convicted when she read the Scriptures, and she didn't want to show it.

"Andrea," said Jamal, "Jesus responded to Peter's confession, not with correction, but by acknowledging its validity and source. Will you please read the next verse?"

"Jesus replied, 'Blessed are you, Simon son of Jonah, for this was not revealed to you by man, but by my Father in heaven.'"[62]

"Scott, will you please read Acts 20:28? You can use my Bible."

"Sure."

As Jamal handed his Bible over, he said, "Scott, because of Paul's extensive rabbinical training, he would be an unlikely person to attribute deity to Jesus, to worship a man from Nazareth and call Him Lord. Isn't that right?"[63]

Scott nodded.

"Keep that in mind as you read what Paul says here."

"Will do," said Scott. "All right, here we go. 'Keep watch over yourselves and all the flock of which the Holy Spirit has made you overseers. Be shepherds of the church of God, which he bought with his own blood.'"

"Thanks, Scott. Whose blood was Paul referring to here?"

Scott continued to read the text to himself. "Hold on a minute. In these verses, why aren't they just calling Jesus 'God' as in G-O-D?"

Jamal responded, "The Jewish community understood these other titles of deity and used them. But Jesus *is* called God, as in G-O-D, in some of these. Scott, will you please read Hebrews 1:8. The writer of Hebrews calls Christ 'God.'"

"No, I'd rather not read. This is ridiculous," said Scott.

"Give me the Bible," said Andrea. "I'll read it. 'But about the Son he says, "Your throne, O God, will last for ever and ever, and righteousness will be the scepter of your kingdom."'"

Andrea handed the Bible back to Jamal. "There you go."

Mina spoke up. "Here's one of my favorites. It's Colossians 2:9. 'For in Christ all the fullness of the Deity lives in bodily form.' And then we have the patron saint of law students, doubting Thomas, who said, 'I won't believe it unless I see the nail wounds in his hands, put my fingers into them, and place my hand into the wound in his side.'"[64]

Nick spoke up. "You know, I can identify with Thomas. Last year I really wanted evidence. I can't stand it when some Christians just believe anything without checking it out. But Thomas motivates me. He was saying, 'Look, it's not every day that someone raises himself from the dead or claims to be God incarnate. If you expect me to believe this, I need a little evidence.'"

Mina continued, "Eight days later, Thomas got his evidence. Listen to this:

Eight days later the disciples were together again, and this time Thomas was with them. The doors were locked; but suddenly, as before, Jesus was standing among them. "Peace be with you," he said. Then he said to Thomas, "Put your finger here, and look at my hands. Put your hand into the wound in my side. Don't be faithless any longer. Believe!"

"My Lord and my God!" Thomas exclaimed.[65]

"Jesus accepted Thomas's acknowledgment of Him as God," observed Mina. "He rebuked Thomas for his unbelief but not for his worship."

As Jamal and Mina talked about the deity of Christ, Andrea felt she was losing a battle she couldn't win. Her friends were intelligent, not just caught up in some emotional religious experience. Their arguments were starting to convince her that Christ was not only divine, but that He backed up His claims through His resurrection. Still, she had questions. If God was so good and powerful, why did He let her cousin die? Why did God allow her parents to divorce? Why did He not stop her former priest from . . .

As her mind wandered, Andrea wondered how life would be different if she placed her trust in Jesus. Would she still be allowed to have fun? What would her family think? Her wandering thoughts were suddenly interrupted.

"Andrea, what do you think?" asked Jamal.

"About what?"

"About Thomas's confession?" asked Jamal.

"Um . . . I guess it's . . . interesting," responded Andrea.

"Well if it isn't Jamal Washington!" yelled a voice from across the room.

Sixteen

DR. INGRAHAM IS NOT PLEASED

EVERYONE TURNED to see an older man in a gray sport coat walking over.

"Hey, Dr. Ingraham," said Brett.

"Hi, Dr. Ingraham," said Lauren. "Your presentation at our atheist club meeting two weeks ago was fascinating."

"Thank you, Lauren. I just hope Mr. Washington here is not indoctrinating you all with his sectarian theology."

Clayton Ingraham smiled at Jamal. "You might have convinced Bill Peterson that Jesus rose from the dead, but you sure aren't convincing me."

Nick's emotions kicked in and he opened his mouth to speak, but Jamal cast him a quick and unmistakable glance. He took a deep breath and closed his mouth.

Without appearing ruffled in the least, Jamal waved his hand and responded graciously, "Dr. Ingraham, I'm thankful that you came over, and I'd like to extend an invitation for you to join us. We meet here every Wednesday evening, and as you came in we were discussing the deity of Christ. Can I buy you a coffee?"

"No thanks. I'm afraid I need to run."

"Well, you're welcome at any time. You and I could share our views and then answer questions. I'm familiar with your positions, and I believe you know where I stand since you've heard me teach."

"Oh, I've heard you all right. You might win some of our undergrads with your emotional appeal, but you certainly won't convince me. Your viewpoint is narrow-minded and intolerant."

You're accusing Jamal of being narrow-minded and intolerant, yet you aren't willing to hear him out? Isn't that intolerance? Andrea thought.

"Dr. Ingraham, would you consider attending Dr. Peterson's upcoming lecture?" asked Mina.

"Everyone is talking about that, aren't they? Bill has been a close friend of mine for many years, so I wouldn't miss this chance to support him. But that doesn't mean I agree with him. Personally, I think his sister's death affected him more than he realizes."

"Dr. Ingraham, I'm glad you'll be there. And don't forget my invitation to join us on Wednesday nights," commented Jamal.

After Dr. Ingraham left, the group continued talking, though the momentum of their discussion was gone. Jamal answered some questions about evil, Old Testament ethics, and the resurrection, then he asked Lauren to share her story and provide a case for her atheism.

Lauren reluctantly agreed, and she explained how she had grown up going to a non-denominational church that taught the Bible verse by verse, but had stopped attending after her parents divorced. She said throughout high school she still prayed on rare occasions, but eventually stopped because it didn't work. It was through studying evolution and anthropology during her sophomore year at Brown that she became convinced that atheism was true. However, she also admitted that she would be open to believing in God if there was compelling evidence.

Mina spoke briefly about indications of design from coding and irreducible complexity within structures of the gene, and Lauren said that appearance of design does not prove God. The conversation lulled, so they said their good-byes and took off.

Later, as Nick was driving Jessica to her apartment, he

spoke up. "I almost blew it when Dr. Ingraham came over to our table."

"Almost, but didn't. Actually, Nick, I appreciate your boldness. He was pretty rude to Jamal, and I know you aren't afraid to speak your mind. I'm usually too intimidated to say anything."

"Jessica, I think Andrea really appreciates your authenticity and kindness. Mina knows so much and answers all her questions, but it seems like Andrea cares what *you* think, even though you don't talk theology as much."

"I love Andrea. I would say more in these discussions, but I just don't have all the answers to her questions. I have learned so much from just listening in. I appreciate you introducing me to Mina and Jamal last year."

"I've learned a ton from them too."

"Hey, did you get the email from Susan Peterson?" asked Jessica.

"About the dessert at their house after Dr. Peterson's lecture?"

"Yeah! I'm so excited to be able to catch up. Mrs. Peterson told me she also invited Andrea. I think I'll call her in a couple days and ask her to join us."

"Great idea."

Seventeen

DR. PETERSON'S LECTURE ON JESUS

NICK AND JESSICA were invited by Dr. Peterson to visit for a few minutes backstage before his lecture. With him were Mrs. Peterson, Jamal, and two reporters who had stopped by to ask Dr. Peterson a few questions. After spending ten minutes with the reporters, Dr. Peterson glanced up and saw a good friend walking toward him. "Clay! How are you?"

Nick forced a quick smile and glanced at Jamal, who wore a genuine smile. *How does he do that?* Nick wondered.

"Well, Bill Peterson, I never thought I'd see this day, but it's great to see you!"

The vice president, Dr. Clark Price,

poked his head in. "Dr. Peterson, the auditorium is packed and it's time for us to begin. I'll be doing the welcome, Dean Sanchez will follow with your biography, and then you'll have approximately seventy minutes for your lecture. Try to wrap up by 8:15 so we can take fifteen minutes of questions."

A few minutes later, Dr. Peterson began. "Thank you for that very warm and gracious introduction. My esteemed colleagues, students, and special guests, I am deeply grateful that you chose to come this evening. During our next few moments together I would like to share from my own academic and personal journey, and more specifically, recount for you how my beliefs about the historical Christ have changed."

As Dr. Peterson started his lecture, Andrea noticed how quiet the room fell. She sat in the third row with Jessica, Nick, and Mina to her left, and Brett, Lauren, and Scott to her right. Even though she knew there would be some disagreement in the audience, she felt that her atheist club friends would respect Dr. Peterson's presentation. She also knew Scott would not hesitate to ask a tough question or two at the end. Andrea wondered what her friends would think if she decided to place her trust in Christ. At this point she thought back to all of her conversations with Jamal, Nick, and Mina, and though not all of her questions were answered, it seemed that the case for Christianity was becoming more compelling than atheism. After reflecting on her own intellectual doubts, she focused on Dr. Peterson's lecture.

"When I was a child, my mother took my sister and me to a Presbyterian church in New York. I initially believed in Christ during my early years, but I became a skeptic in graduate school as I became disturbed by the variances in the papyri manuscripts, or copies of the New Testament. As a student, I felt frustrated by the evil and injustice of the world, and asked myself why God would allow such evil. Looking back, I believe the philosophers I studied, such as Immanuel Kant, began to affect my views. I questioned whether we can know anything beyond the physical world. I was left with an agnostic view of God and told myself that if He existed, He was probably deistic, not all-powerful, and probably unable to solve the problem of evil. For a few years, I even turned to atheism and tried to turn my students against God. I would talk about the evils of Old Testament ethics, the hard sayings of Jesus, and killings led by religious people.

"Although I struggled with the so-called problem of evil, it was actually the admission of objectivity in evil and morality that began pointing me back to God several years ago. I wrestled with all of the various forms of ethics— quantitative and qualitative utilitarianism, relativism, as well as forms of deontological ethics—and I discovered that the best explanation for objective morality was to believe in a god who is the standard of all moral laws.

"Also a few years ago, after several conversations with an atheist philosopher friend who had turned away from atheism, I took time to study the theory of Intelligent Design from authors such as Francis Collins, William Dembski, Jonathan Wells, and Michael Behe. I began to admit probability in intelligent design. However, I was still skeptical of the Scriptures and miracles in the New Testament.

"Unfortunately, not only did I experience doubts, but I continued to attack the beliefs of any Christian I came across. It was because of me that my wife stopped attending church. Not only that, but I convinced hundreds, if not thousands, of students to question the authority of Scripture. I fear I have undermined the faith of many. Actually, I know I have.

"Last winter, when I learned my sister Barbara had a brain tumor, I took a leave of absence from teaching and had my assistant, Jamal Washington, fill in for several of my classes. After taking multiple trips out to Portland, my wife and I decided to remain out there with my sister until she died.

"Those of you who knew my sister know that she not only believed in God, but she lived out her Christian faith. Nor was her faith blind. I remember Barbara reading N. T. Wright's scholarly work on the resurrection and wanting to debate me on the subject. I knew I wouldn't stand a chance against her."

Several in the audience chuckled, and Dr. Peterson paused for a moment.

"At her funeral, I began to think more intentionally about the possibility of heaven and the implications of the resurrection on the afterlife. I was saddened by her passing, and the minister spoke on Paul's words to the church of the Thessalonians. 'We don't grieve like those who have no hope,' he said,[66] and as I listened, I wondered whether or not I had any hope.

"At the end of the funeral, I was surprised to see one of my students in attendance. Nick was a freshman last year and had a voracious appetite for learning. Although he grew up going to church, he had drifted from believing in the deity of Christ largely because of my teaching. Thankfully, Nick wasn't satisfied with my objections to Christianity. He investigated my claims on his own and eventually came back to the faith. Not only that, he had the gall to show up at my sister's funeral and tell me that Jesus Christ loved me and died for me. Picture that, if you will. A freshman with no real theological training challenging *me*—a tenured professor of thirty years—to be intellectually open to the idea of the resurrection and afterlife! I didn't care to admit it at the time, but his challenge lit a fire in me. For two months straight I reinvestigated everything. I reevaluated believing in God's existence and the possibility of miracles, and I spent time refreshing my research and reconsidering the variances in the manuscripts. Finally, I had no choice but to acknowledge that the New Testament is historically true.

"Tonight I want to share why I believe the testimony about Jesus Christ in the gospels and writings of the New Testament is trustworthy."

Dr. Peterson lectured passionately on the reliability of Scripture in regard to the abundance and early dating of the manuscripts of the gospels. As he did, Nick took Jessica's hand. He knew she had been praying for Dr. Peterson and that she was probably praying silently for Andrea as he spoke. Jessica had winked at Nick when Dr. Peterson mentioned his name.

Eighteen

JESUS AND HIS FATHER

AFTER TWENTY MINUTES of speaking about the trustworthiness of the New Testament, Dr. Peterson listed multiple references to Christ's claims of deity throughout the Bible. He also explored the evidence of Christ's resurrection. Andrea took note that some of it seemed similar to what Jamal was teaching. Dr. Peterson continued lecturing with a sense of conviction and authority that had never before been seen in his lectures.

"In the gospel of John we have a confrontation between Jesus and a group of Jewish leaders. It's triggered by Jesus curing a lame man on the Sabbath. Jews were forbidden to do any work on the

Sabbath, so the Jewish leaders harassed Him for breaking the Sabbath rules. 'My Father is always working, and so am I,' Jesus replied, so 'the Jewish leaders tried all the harder to find a way to kill him. For he not only broke the Sabbath, he called God his Father, thereby making himself equal with God.'"[67]

Dr. Peterson looked at Dr. Clayton Ingraham and some of the faculty in the front row. "Some of my colleagues might say, 'Look, Bill, I can't see how this proves anything. Jesus called God His Father. So what? All Christians call God their Father, but this doesn't mean they are claiming to be God.'[68]

"The Jews of Jesus' time heard in His words a meaning that is easily lost to us now. Whenever we study a document, we must take into account the language, the culture, and especially the person or persons the document addresses. In this case, the culture is Jewish, and the persons being addressed are Jewish religious leaders. And something about what Jesus said really got under their skin. The text says, 'So the Jewish leaders tried all the harder to find a way to kill him. For he not only broke the Sabbath, he called God his Father, thereby making himself equal with God.'"[69]

Dr. Peterson again spoke directly to Dr. Ingraham and the faculty. "What could He have said to cause such a drastic reaction? Many of you disagree with what I'm saying this evening, yet you're hopefully not trying to find a way to kill me! At least not *all* of you . . ." He paused to smile while several chuckled, then continued. "Let's look at the passage and see how the Jews understood Jesus' remarks more than two thousand years ago in their own culture.[70]

"Their problem was that Jesus said, '*my* Father,' not '*our* Father.' By the rules of their language, Jesus' use of this phrase was a claim to be equal with God. The Jews rarely referred to God as 'my Father.' Or if they did, they would always qualify the statement by adding the phrase 'in heaven.' However, Jesus did not add the phrase. He made a claim the Jews could not misinterpret when He called God 'my Father.'[71]

"Not only did Jesus claim equality with God as His Father, but He also asserted that He was one with the Father. During the Feast of the Dedication of Jerusalem, some of the other Jewish leaders approached Jesus and questioned Him about whether He was the Christ. Jesus concluded His comments to them by saying, 'The Father and I are one.'[72] How did they respond to that? 'Once again the people picked up stones to kill him. Jesus said, "At my Father's direction I have done many good works. For which one are you going to stone me?"'[73]

"Now some of you might wonder why the Jews reacted so strongly to what Jesus said about being *one* with the Father. The structure of the phrase in the Greek gives us an answer. A. T. Robertson, the foremost Greek scholar of his day, wrote that in the Greek, the word *one* in this passage is neuter, not masculine, and does not indicate one in person or purpose but rather one in 'essence of nature.' Robertson then adds, 'This crisp statement is the climax of Christ's claims about the relationship between the Father and himself. They stir the Pharisees to uncontrollable anger.'"[74]

Nineteen

WHO DO YOU SAY I AM?

DR. PETERSON RAISED his voice and looked directly at those in the room. "My friends, Jesus Christ claimed to be God, and to Him it is of fundamental importance that men and women believe Him to be who He was. Either we believe Him, or we don't. He didn't leave us any wiggle room for in-between, watered down alternatives. Based on what Jesus claimed about Himself, if His claims were not true, you couldn't call Him either a good moral man or a great prophet. Those options aren't open to us, and Jesus never intended them to be.

"Since we have already established the historicity of the gospels in the New

Testament, we rule out the possibility of Christ being legend. We now go to the famous words of C. S. Lewis, former professor at Cambridge University, and a former agnostic himself. He wrote:"

> I am trying to prevent anyone saying the really foolish thing that people often say about Him: 'I'm reading to accept Jesus as a great moral teacher, but I don't accept His claim to be God.' That is the one thing we must not say. A man who was merely a man and said the sort of things Jesus said would not be a great moral teacher. He would either be a lunatic—on a level with the man who says he is a poached egg—or else he would be the Devil of Hell. You must make your choice. Either this man was, and is, the Son of God, or else a madman or something worse. . . .
>
> You can shut Him up for a fool, you can spit at Him and kill Him as a demon, or you can fall at His feet and call Him Lord and God. But let us not come up with any patronizing nonsense about his being a great human teacher. He has not left that open to us. He did not intend to.[75]

Dr. Peterson turned the page of his notes and said, "In the words of Kenneth Scott Latourette, historian of Christianity at Yale University,"

It is not his teachings which make Jesus so remarkable, although these would be enough to give him distinction. It is a combination of the teachings with the man himself. The two cannot be separated. . . . It must be obvious to any thoughtful reader of the Gospel records that Jesus regarded himself and his message as inseparable. He was a great teacher, but he was more. His teachings about the kingdom of God, about human conduct, and about God were important, but they could not be divorced from him without, from his standpoint, being vitiated.[76]

Dr. Peterson continued, "Jesus claimed to be God. His claim must be either true or false, and everyone should give it the same consideration He expected of His disciples when He put the question to them, 'Who do you say I am?'"[77]

Twenty

WAS JESUS A LIAR?

"**LADIES AND GENTLEMEN,** if the claims of Jesus were false, then we have only two alternatives. He either knew they were false, or He didn't. We will consider each possibility separately and examine the evidence for it.

"If, when Jesus made His claims, He knew that He was not God, then He was lying and deliberately deceiving His followers. But if He was a liar, then He was also a hypocrite because He taught others to be honest at whatever cost. Worse than that, if He was lying, He was evil because He told others to trust Him for their eternal destiny. Finally, He would also be a fool because His claims of being God—claims He could

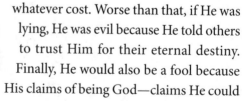

have backed away from to save Himself even at the last minute—led to His crucifixion. However, historically, we know that the character of Christ was impeccable. Even His enemies praised His character. Pilate said, 'I find no fault in this man.'"[78]

Mina looked down the row of students and noticed Andrea taking notes.

Dr. Peterson adjusted his glasses. "William Lecky, one of Great Britain's most noted historians and a fierce opponent of organized Christianity, saw the effect of true Christianity on the world. He wrote,"

It was reserved for Christianity to present to the world an ideal which though all the changes of eighteen centuries has inspired the hearts of men with an impassioned love; has shown itself capable of acting on all ages, nations, temperaments, and conditions; has been not only the highest pattern of virtue, but the strongest incentive to its practice. . . . The simple record of these three short years of active life has done more to regenerate and soften mankind than all the disquisitions of philosophers and all the exhortations of moralists.[79]

As Dr. Peterson spoke, Andrea was silently praying, "Jesus, I now know that You're for real. Please forgive me.

I do believe in You and I will trust You with my life." She held back her emotions and continued to listen.

Dr. Peterson set his eyes on the rows directly behind Andrea where several students were wearing atheist T-shirts. "You know, many of the 'New Atheists' avoid the historical case for the reliability of the New Testament. For example, in Christopher Hitchens' chapter 'The Evil of the New Testament,' he provides no strong arguments against the historicity of the New Testament. How can you call the New Testament *evil*? Christ is the most compassionate teacher in history. Hitchens fails to refute this fact. He simply mentions some alleged contradictions and repeats Bart Ehrman's popular-level work that mentions that a portion of Mark 8 is not in the original.[80] Christian theologians have admitted this for years! By the way, Ehrman didn't discover that idea on his own. He probably learned it from an evangelical! His evangelical mentor, Bruce Metzger, a textual critic, testified that the copies of the New Testament we have now resemble the original to an extremely high percentage. And if Ehrman wants to be intellectually honest with the conclusions of his academic textual criticism, he also needs to admit the very high accuracy of the New Testament copies we have today."

With this statement, many in the audience broke out in applause, though the row of atheists and a number of professors refrained. Jessica glanced beside her and was surprised to see Andrea clapping.

"It is extremely illogical to think that Jesus Christ is a liar. Historian Philip Schaff said,"

How in the name of logic, common sense, and experience, could an imposter—that is a deceitful, selfish, depraved man—have invented, and consistently maintained from the beginning to end, the purest and noblest character known in history with the most perfect air of truth and reality? How could he have conceived and carried out a plan of unparalleled beneficence, moral magnitude, and sublimity, and sacrificed his own life for it, in the face of the strongest prejudices of his people and age?[81]

Twenty-One

WAS JESUS
A LUNATIC?

"**SOMEONE WHO LIVED** as Jesus lived, taught as Jesus taught, and died as Jesus died could not have been a liar. Let's look at other alternatives. If we find it inconceivable that Jesus was a liar, then couldn't He actually have mistakenly thought Himself to be God? After all, it's possible to be both sincere and wrong. But we must remember that for someone to mistakenly think himself God, especially in the context of a fiercely monotheistic culture, and then to tell others that their eternal destiny depended on believing in him, is no small flight of fancy. It takes a raving lunatic to think such a thing. Is it possible that Jesus Christ was deranged?"[82]

"Yes!" yelled one of the students with a red atheist shirt.

"No, I'm afraid it's not," continued Dr. Peterson, remaining calm. "Today we would treat someone who believes himself to be God the same way we would treat someone who believes he is Napoleon. We would see him as deluded and self-deceived. We would hope he wouldn't hurt himself or anyone else. Yet in Jesus we don't observe the abnormalities and imbalances that accompany such derangement. If He was insane, His poise and composure was nothing short of amazing.[83]

"Let me read an observation from psychologist Gary R. Collins."

Jesus was loving but didn't let his compassion immobilize him; he didn't have a bloated ego, even though he was often surrounded by adoring crowds; he maintained balance despite an often demanding lifestyle; he always knew what he was doing and where he was going; he cared deeply about people, including women and children, who weren't seen as important back then; he was able to accept people while not merely winking at their sin; he responded to individuals based on where they were at and what they uniquely needed. All in all, I just don't see signs that Jesus was suffering from any known mental illness. . . . He was much healthier than anyone else I know—including me![84]

Dr. Peterson looked up from his notes and said, "I cannot personally conclude that Jesus was a liar or a lunatic. The only alternative is that He was—and is—the Christ, the Son of God, as He claimed. But in spite of the logic and evidence, many people cannot seem to bring themselves to this conclusion. My desire is that you would change your mind and trust in Christ right now as your Savior and Lord. Tonight, I want to ask for forgiveness from everyone that I've led astray in my many years of teaching here at Opal University. My academic pride kept me from honestly examining the truth claims of Christ and the gospel writers. It was also my pride that kept me from acknowledging Christ as Lord of my life. I think I basically wanted to run my own life and be my own god. Today, I want you to reconsider the true Jesus who is revealed in Scripture.[85]

"Two months ago, my wife Susan and I each confessed our sin and accepted Jesus Christ's atoning death as the payment for our sin. We also confessed Him as the Lord of our lives. If you don't know Jesus Christ, I encourage you to place your trust in Him right now. It is the wisest decision you will ever make.

"And now *my* time is up and it's time for *your* questions."

The audience applauded, with about half of them standing to their feet. Including Andrea.

Twenty-Two

QUESTIONS FROM ATHEISTS AND SKEPTICS

AS THE AUDIENCE was cheering, Vice President Price walked up the center aisle with a microphone and said, "We are going to take a few questions from the audience."

Scott was the first to ask a question. "Dr. Peterson, I've heard that it was Constantine who brought pressure to upgrade Christ's status to deity in the fourth century's Council of Nicaea."

Scott returned to his seat and Dr. Peterson leaned into the microphone.

"Have you been reading Dan Brown novels?" Dr. Peterson asked, as several people throughout the auditorium chuckled. Dr. Peterson continued, "Here is the case I've provided tonight. The New Testament was composed in the first century, just decades after the events surrounding Jesus. The books of the New Testament predate the Council of Nicaea by more than two centuries. Though written by different people for a variety of purposes, they share one unmistakable theme. Jesus Christ is God."

An older man with a beard asked the next question. "Dr. Peterson, can you provide any sources outside the Bible to show that Jesus Christ was considered God?"

"Certainly. The ante-Nicene fathers provide additional support that Jesus was considered divine. I have documented some of their quotes. Ignatius of Antioch in AD 110 wrote, 'God is incarnate . . . God himself appearing in the form of man.'[86] Justin Martyr, who lived from AD 100–165, said of Christ, '. . . being the First-begotten Word of God, is even God.'[87] Irenaeus, AD 177, declared, '. . . the Father is God and the Son is God; for He who is born of God is God.' Melito of Sardis wrote, around AD 177, that Jesus was a man, yet He is God."[88]

Dr. Peterson continued, "Probably the most convincing evidence that Jesus was considered divine before Nicaea comes from non-Christian writers. The Greek satirist Lucian of Samosata (c. AD 170), the Roman philosopher Celsus (c. 177), and the Roman governor Pliny the Younger (c. 112) make it clear that early Christians understood Jesus as divine. Pliny persecuted Christians because of their belief that Jesus was divine. Let me read a statement that I documented coming from Pliny. 'They had met regularly before dawn on a fixed day to chant verses alternately among themselves in honour of Christ as if to a god.'"[89]

Twenty-Three

CAN YOU PROVE IT TO ME SCIENTIFICALLY?

AFTER SEVERAL more questions, Lauren, Andrea's friend, took the microphone and spoke forcefully, "Hi, my name is Lauren. I'm just wondering . . . all of this stuff about God, Jesus, and the resurrection. Can you prove it to me scientifically?"

Dr. Peterson just said, "No, I can't."

Andrea could hear chuckling behind her from her atheist friends. Her friend Sam, sitting a couple rows behind her, yelled, "Then don't talk to us about it! You religious people have nothing but blind faith!"

Dr. Peterson smiled at the comments and calmly began speaking. "Scientific proof is based on showing that something is a fact by repeating the event in the presence of the person questioning the fact. It is done in a controlled environment where observations can be made, data collected, and hypotheses empirically verified."[90]

"Do you really know anything about science?" yelled another student.

"Well, I'm not a scientist, but I might know more than you think. I did consider pursuing the field as a career when I double-majored in physics and biology as an undergraduate at Harvard, and I still read several scientific journals for pleasure. Testing the truth of a hypothesis by the use of controlled experiments is one of the key techniques of the modern scientific method. For example, someone claims that Ivory soap doesn't float. I claim it does float, so to prove my point, I take the doubter to the kitchen, put eight inches of water in the sink at 82.7 degrees, and drop in the soap. *Plunk!* We make observations, we draw data, and we verify my hypothesis empirically: Ivory soap floats."[91]

Dr. Peterson continued, "If the scientific method were the only method we had for proving facts, you couldn't prove that you had lunch today. There's no way you could repeat that event in a controlled situation. Thankfully, the other method of proof, the *legal-historical method*, is based on showing that something is a fact beyond reasonable doubt. In other words, we reach a verdict on the weight of the evidence and have no rational basis for doubting the decision. Legal-historical proof depends on three kinds of testimony: oral testimony, written testimony, and exhibits (such as a gun, a bullet, or a notebook). Using the legal-historical method to determine the facts, you could prove beyond a reasonable doubt that you went to lunch today. Your friends saw you there, the waiter remembers seeing you, you have the restaurant receipt, and there's a stain on your shirt.[92]

"Lauren, the scientific method can be used to prove only repeatable things. It isn't adequate for proving or disproving questions about persons or events in history. The scientific method isn't appropriate for answering such questions as, *Did Abraham Lincoln live? Was Martin Luther King Jr. a civil rights leader? Who was Jesus of Nazareth? Was Christopher Columbus a real person? Was Jesus Christ raised from the dead?* These questions are outside the realm of scientific proof, and we must place them in the realm of legal-historical proof.[93] Thank you."

Again the students applauded.

Dr. Price walked to the podium, shook Dr. Peterson's hand, and thanked him for giving his lecture. This had been one of the most surprising and stimulating speaking events the school had experienced in recent years.

Twenty-Four

GOOD NEWS AT THE PETERSONS'

ABOUT AN HOUR LATER, some twenty students and several members of the faculty were sitting outside of the Petersons' house celebrating Dr. Peterson's lecture. Dr. Peterson asked his wife to share her story, and the students warmed to her kind personality. She said that the love of God compelled her to come to faith in Christ. The students listened intently as she shared that her spiritual journey was not as intensely intellectual as Dr. Peterson's. For her, she felt a conviction of her selfishness and sensed that God was pursuing a relationship with her. He loved her.

To everyone's surprise, Andrea spoke

up when Mrs. Peterson had finished. "I feel like I need to thank not only the Petersons, but also Jessica, Mina, Jamal, and Nick for being so patient with me and showing God's love to me. I want you all to know that tonight, as Dr. Peterson was speaking, I placed my trust in Jesus."

After her words, Jamal led with a loud cheer as Mina and Jessica hugged Andrea.

Brett, who felt uncomfortable with all these Christians around him who seemed to have such assurance about God and affection for each other, still had reservations. *There's a lot of what these people say that makes sense, but I'm not about to jump into this faith thing without a lot more time to investigate and think it through.*

"I want to thank you all too," said Brett politely. "I've been a professing atheist pretty much my whole life, but because of your intellectual reasons, along with insights I've learned from Jamal, I am now beginning to believe that Christ actually lived. But . . . I'm just not ready to become a religious Christian like Andrea. I still have plenty of doubts—especially about the resurrection."

"Like what?" asked Dr. Peterson.

"Um . . . I really don't want to talk about it now. After all, I'm outnumbered." He smiled, and so did Dr. Peterson.

"I understand, Brett. If you ever want to talk, please call me or stop by my office."

"Thanks," responded Brett. "I just might take you up on that offer . . . sometime."

The Coffeehouse Chronicles series includes:

Is the Bible True . . . Really?
Who Is Jesus . . . Really?
Did the Resurrection Happen . . . Really?

NOTES

1. Colossians 1:15–20

2. Video testimony found on www.iamsecond.com; used by permission.

3. Christopher Hitchens, *God Is Not Great: How Religion Poisons Everything* (New York: Hachette, 2007), 111.

4. Bertrand Russell, *Why I Am Not a Christian* (New York: Simon & Schuster, 1957), 16.

5. Hitchens, *God Is Not Great*, 114.

6. Dinesh D'Souza, *What's So Great about Christianity* (Washington, DC: Regnery, 2007), 296.

7. 1 Corinthians 15:14

8. Otto Betz, *What Do We Know about Jesus?* (Norwich, U.K.: SCM Press, 1968), 9.

9. D'Souza, *What's So Great about Christianity*, 296.

10. Ibid., 295.

11. Richard Dawkins, *The God Delusion* (New York: Houghton Mifflin, 2006), 51.

12. D'Souza, *What's So Great about Christianity*, 218.

13. *Hitler's Table Talk* (New York: Enigma Books, 2000). Quoted by D'Souza, *What's So Great about Christianity*, 218.

14. Adolf Hitler, *Mein Kampf* (Boston: Houghton Mifflin, 1999), 65. Quoted by D'Souza, *What's So Great about Christianity*, 217.

15. Adapted from content in D. James Kennedy and Jerry Newcombe, *What If Jesus Had Never Been Born?* (Nashville: Thomas Nelson, 1994).

16. For more information on the trustworthiness of the New Testament, see Book One in this Coffeehouse Chronicles series, *Is the Bible True . . . Really?*

17. Thomas Paine, *Collected Writings*, ed. Eric Foner (New York: The Library of America, 1995), 9.

18. F. F. Bruce, T*he New Testament Documents: Are They Reliable?* (Downers Grove, IL: InterVarsity Press, 1972), 119.

19. Gary R. Habermas, *The Verdict of History* (Nashville: Thomas Nelson, 1988), 87.

20. Ibid.

21. Cornelius Tacitus, *Annals* (Chicago: William Benton, 1952), XV, 44.

22. Lucian of Samosata, *The Death of Peregrine,* in *The Works of Lucian of Samosata*, 4 vols., trans. H. W. Fowler and F. G. Fowler (Oxford: The Clarendon Press, 1949), 11–13.

23. Ibid.

24. Lucian, "Life of Claudius," in *The Works of Lucian of Samosata*, 25.4.

25. Suetonius, *Lives of the Caesars*, 26.2.

26. Pliny the Younger, *Epistles* X.

27. Ibid.

28. Habermas, *The Verdict of History*, 93.

29. Julius Africanus, *Chronography*, 18.1.

30. Bruce, *The New Testament Documents*, 113.

31. Ibid., 123.

32. Habermas, *The Verdict of History*, 119.

33. "For I received from the Lord what I also passed on to you: The Lord Jesus, on the night he was betrayed, took bread, and when he had given thanks, he broke it and said, 'This is my body, which is for you; do this in remembrance of me'" (1 Corinthians 11:23–24).

34. Habermas, *The Verdict of History*, 121.

35. 1 Corinthians 15:3–5 NASB

36. 1 Corinthians 15:11 NASB

37. David Hume, *Enquiries Concerning Human Understanding and Concerning the Principles of Morals*, 3rd ed. (Oxford: The Clarendon Press, 1992), 144–146, 14.

38. Ronald H. Nash, *Faith and Reason* (Grand Rapids: Zondervan, 1988), 230.

39. Norman L. Geisler, *Miracles and the Modern Mind* (Grand Rapids: Baker, 1992), 27–28.

40. Ibid.

41. Geisler, *Miracles and the Modern Mind*, quoted by R. Douglas Geivett and Gary Habermas (Downers Grove, IL: InterVarsity Press, 1997), 78–79.

42. Nash, *Faith and Reason*, 234.

43. Matthew 10:32–33

44. Mark 2:5 NLT; see also Luke 7:48–50

45. Isaiah 43:25

46. Mark 2:7 NLT

47. Lewis Sperry Chafer, *Systematic Theology* (Dallas: Dallas Theological Seminary Press, 1947), 5:21.

48. Matthew 4:10 NLT

49. Robert M. Bowman and J. Ed Komoszewski, *Putting Jesus in His Place: The Case for the Deity of Christ* (Grand Rapids: Kregel, 2007), 246–47.

50. Mark 14:60–64, italics added

51. Josh McDowell and Sean McDowell, *More Than a Carpenter* (Carol Stream, IL: Tyndale, 2009), 19–20.

52. Mark 14:63

53. McDowell and McDowell, *More Than a Carpenter*, 22.

54. Robert Anderson, *The Lord from Heaven* (London: James Nisbet, 1910), 5.

55. Matthew 27:43

56. Henry Barclay Swete, *The Gospel According to St. Mark* (London: Macmillan, 1898), 339.

57. Irwin H. Linton, *The Sanhedrin Verdict* (New York: Loizeaux Bros., 1943), 7.

58. Matthew 27:41–43 NLT

59. McDowell and McDowell, *More Than a Carpenter*, 10.

60. Titus 2:13 KJV

61. Matthew 4:10 NLT

62. Matthew 16:17

63. McDowell and McDowell, *More Than a Carpenter*, 12.

64. John 20:25 NLT

65. John 20:26–28 NLT

66. See 1 Thessalonians 4:13

67. See John 5:16–18 NLT

68. McDowell and McDowell, *More Than a Carpenter*, 14.

69. John 5:18 NLT

70. McDowell and McDowell, *More Than a Carpenter*, 14.

71. Ibid., 15.

72. John 10:30 NLT

73. John 10:31–32 NLT

74. Archibald Thomas Robertson, *Word Pictures in the New Testament* (New York: Harper & Brothers, 1932), 5:186.

75. C. S. Lewis, *Mere Christianity* (New York: Macmillan, 1960), 40–41.

76. Kenneth Scott Latourette, *A History of the Christianity* (New York: Harper & Row, 1953), 44, 48.

77. Matthew 16:15 NLT

78. McDowell and McDowell, *More Than a Carpenter*, 30.

79. William E. Lecky, *History of European Morals from Augustus to Charlemagne* (New York: D. Appleton, 1903), 2:8–9.

80. Hitchens, *God Is Not Great*, 120–21.

81. Philip Schaff, *The Person of Christ* (New York: American Tract Society, 1913), 94–95.

82. McDowell and McDowell, *More Than a Carpenter*, 33.

83. Ibid.

84. Gary R. Collins, quoted in Lee Strobel, *The Case for Christ* (Grand Rapids: Zondervan, 1988), 147.

85. McDowell and McDowell, *More Than a Carpenter*, 36.

86. James A. Kliest, *The Epistles of St. Clement of Rome and St. Ignatius of Antioch,* "To the Ephesians" (Ramsey: Paulist Press, 1978).

87. Alexander Roberts, *The Ante-Nicene Fathers*, vol. I (Grand Rapids: Eerdmans, 1993), 184.

88. Joseph P. Smith, *St. Irenaeus: Proof of the Apostolic Preaching* (Ramsey: Paulist Press, 1978), chap. 47.

89. Pliny, *Letters and Panegyricus*, trans. Betty Radice, Loeb Classical Library (Cambridge: Harvard University Press, 1969), 10.96 (2.289).

90. McDowell and McDowell, *More Than a Carpenter*, 42.

91. Ibid., 43.

92. Ibid.

93. Ibid.

ACKNOWLEDGMENTS

WE WOULD LIKE to thank Randall Payleitner, our acquisitions editor at Moody Publishers, for his extensive work and outstanding services to help make this book possible. Also, we thank Paul Santhouse for his excellent editing, and Clay Sterrett (Dave's father) and Melissa Kibby for reading the initial manuscript and providing feedback, corrections, and encouragement.

The authors are grateful for permission to use the following copyrighted material:

Excerpts from *More Than a Carpenter*, by Josh McDowell and Sean McDowell, © 2009 by Josh McDowell and Sean McDowell. Used by permission of Tyndale House Publishers.

Excerpts from *The New Evidence That Demands a Verdict*, by Josh McDowell, ©1999 by Josh McDowell. Used by permission of Thomas Nelson Publishers.

The Coffee House Chronicles

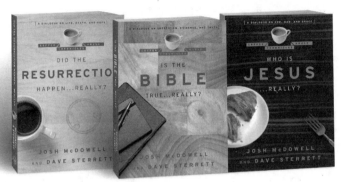

ISBN-13: 978-0-8024-8768-1

ISBN-13: 978-0-8024-8766-7

ISBN-13: 978-0-8024-8767-4

With over 40 million books sold, bestselling author Josh McDowell is no stranger to creatively presenting biblical truth. Now, partnering with fellow apologist Dave Sterrett, Josh introduces a new series targeted at the intersection of story and truth.

The Coffee House Chronicles are short, easily devoured novellas aimed at answering prevalent spiritual questions. Each book in the series tackles a long-contested question of the faith, and then answers these questions with truth through relationships and dialogue in each story.

MOODY
PUBLISHERS

www.MoodyPublishers.com

Why Trust Jesus?

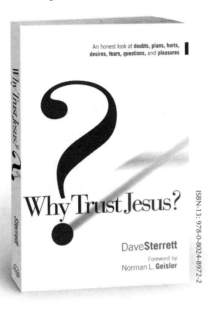

Our generation is up for grabs! Our trust has been shattered in other areas as we have seen hypocrisy in governmental leaders as well as in the church. We are looking for relationships that are authentic and full of life, but we have many questions in regard to faith, reason, suffering and even the person of Jesus himself.

www.MoodyPublishers.com

Just Do Something

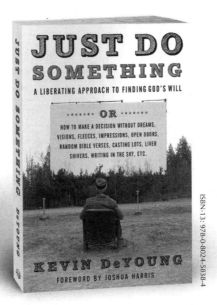

Hyperspiritual approaches to finding God's will just don't work. It's time to try something new: give up. God doesn't need to tell us what to do at each fork in the road. He's already revealed His plan for our lives: to love Him with our whole hearts, to obey His Word, and after that, to do what we like. No need for hocus-pocus. No reason to be directionally challenged. *Just Do Something.*

MOODY
PUBLISHERS

www.MoodyPublishers.com

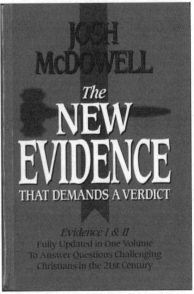